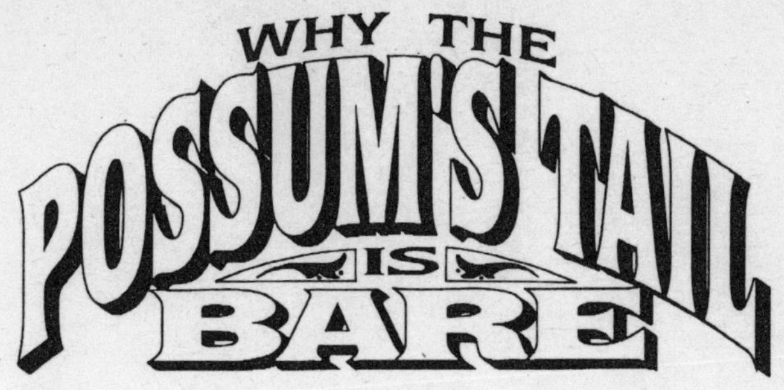

And Other Classic Southern Stories

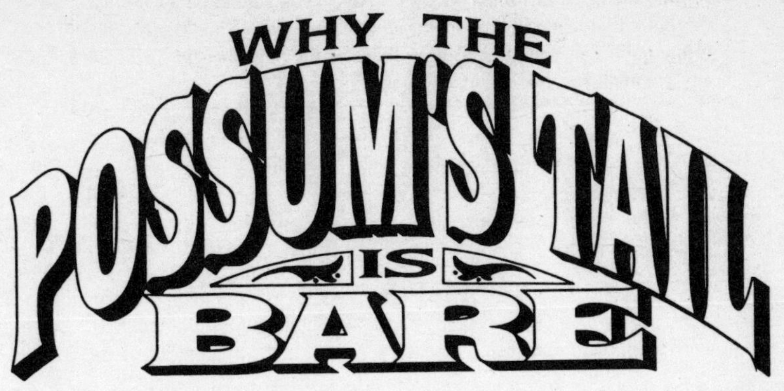

And Other Classic Southern Stories

Selected and compiled by

Jimmy Neil Smith

WHY THE POSSUM'S TAIL IS BARE is an original publication of Avon Books. This work has never before appeared in book form.

AVON BOOKS
A division of
The Hearst Corporation
1350 Avenue of the Americas
New York, New York 10019

Cover illustration by Debbie Drechsler
Inside cover author photograph by Tom Pardue
Published by arrangement with the author
Library of Congress Catalog Card Number: 93–90338
ISBN: 0–380–76857–7

First Avon Books Trade Printing: October 1993

Printed in the U.S.A.

OPM 10 9 8 7 6 5 4 3 2 1

In Appreciation

To storyteller and educator Sheila Dailey
for her skilled research and wise counsel

To writer and editor Mary Weaver
for her capable editorial assistance and advice

To Jane Hillhouse and her staff
for their efficient administrative support

To the storytellers and collectors, living or dead,
who have contributed to this volume

Contents

How Things Got to Be the Way They Are

Tricksters and Fools

Introduction

I WAS BORN IN THE HEART OF SOUTHERN APPALACHIA—IN Jonesborough, tucked in the northeastern corner of Tennessee, just a stone's throw from the storied mountains of western North Carolina, southwest Virginia, and eastern Kentucky. Yet growing up, I was unaware of the rich storytelling tradition just outside my door.

Don't misunderstand. My early life was filled with storybooks, and my most memorable school experience is of my eighth-grade teacher, Sarah Keys, reading to use from her favorite childhood book, *Miss Minerva and William Green Hill*. And as a child my favorite time was that spent sitting around the dinner table with my family, long after the dishes were washed and put away, sharing stories.

What I didn't know was that in that time and place, stories of all kinds—folk tales, fairy tales, legends—were swirling all around me. For, you see, these mountains are peopled with natural storytellers who regale anyone who'll listen with tales from America's bountiful oral culture.

I began to discover the Southern storytelling tradition one day in 1972 when I, then teaching high-school journalism, was traveling with my students to a nearby town to print the school newspaper. We were listening to the car radio when storyteller Jerry Clower began telling a tale about coon hunting in his native Mississippi. We listened, and as the story unfolded, we started to chuckle. In the wake of the laughter, I wondered aloud: "Wouldn't it be nice if we could bring storytellers from throughout the United States to tell stories here in Jonesborough?"

Though our thoughts that day soon turned elsewhere, we had been captivated by the simple telling of a tale. For me the moment had been an epiphany, and it would change my life. The experience teased me, wouldn't let me go. By October of the following year I had created the National Storytelling Festival—an annual event, now twenty years old, that has been the catalyst for a renewed appreciation of the art of storytelling throughout America.

During the past two decades I have had the opportunity and the pleasure of exploring this country's abundant treasury of stories—stories I want to share with you in *Why the Possum's Tail Is Bare*. It is, quite simply, a collection of tales from America's Southland. Some are classics, some are less familiar, some are Southern-flavored versions of well-known tales.

This book does not pretend to be scholarly or comprehensive. It is instead an excursion through some of the South's best oral literature: simple tales, each highly narrative, presented not in literary fashion but the way the tales were told, directly from the oral tradition. As you read through this volume, you'll get to know the stories that form the bedrock of the South's cultural legacy and the characters who people them.

You'll meet Jack—the same fellow who climbed the beanstalk—in meandering tales about a mountain boy who battles giants, suffers the trials and tribulations of seeking his fortune, and, luckily for him, triumphs over them all.

You'll meet talking animals like Br'er Rabbit, that wily creature who by cunning and sheer perseverance always outsmarts his more powerful foes.

You'll meet America's first storytellers, the Native

Americans, who, without scientific theories, told tales to explain the unexplainable—to account for the mysteries of the universe or reveal why the possum's tail is bare.

You'll meet Pretty Polly, a brave, quick-witted woman who solves a Southern Appalachian murder mystery. And Snow Bella, Snow White's Cajun cousin, who after surviving her wicked stepmother's devious plots managed to marry her Prince Charming. And Spear-finger, the gruesome creature of Cherokee lore who traveled all over the Southern mountains, always hungry, looking for someone to stab with her long, bony forefinger.

Only the Native American stories are indigenous to the South. The others arrived here by way of the tinker's camps of Scotland, the tribal villages of Africa, the settlements of Acadia, and the many other places that were home to those transplanted to this region. The travelers brought their stories with them to their new land, and the South, like the rest of this country, became a melting pot of storytelling.

I hope that you'll find each of this volume's stories an enriching opportunity to become better acquainted with some of the South's favorite characters, enduring values, and unique flavor. For today it is such stories—and those cherished in every other corner of America—that remind us who we are, connect us to our rich and diverse oral tradition, and in this competitive, computerized world, keep us in touch with our humanity.

—JONESBOROUGH, TENNESSEE
FEBRUARY 1993

Tales of Wonder and Magic

Snow Bella

A Louisiana version of "Snow White" that was originally told in French

ONCE THERE WERE TWO SISTERS SITTING NEAR THE FIREplace as snow was falling outside. While at her sewing, one of the sisters looked out at the snow through the window and suddenly stuck her finger with her needle. She pressed her finger, hurt by the sting of the needle, and a drop of red, red blood fell on her dress.

"You should make a wish," said the other sister, "and it will be granted for your having lost a drop of blood."

"Then I wish," began the sister, "that someday I shall have a most beautiful daughter, whose cheeks and lips will be as red as this blood and whose skin will be as white as the snow falling outside."

It turned out just as the sister had wished. She married a very handsome young man and had a girl whose lips and cheeks were deep red like the blood that had dropped from her finger and whose skin was as fair and white as the snow. She was so beautiful that her mother called her Snow Bella.

However, Snow Bella's mother, the sister who had lost the drop of blood while sewing when it snowed, became ill and suddenly died. Her husband was married again to a very cruel and wicked woman who became Snow Bella's stepmother. The stepmother vainly thought herself very beautiful, and no sooner was she married than she became violently jealous of Snow Bella's great beauty. So she treated the girl most cruelly, making her do all the housework. She also began plotting and planning a way to get rid of her stepdaughter.

"Snow Bella," said the cruel stepmother one day, "come with me into the woods. We shall look around for some herbs and roots for my skin."

So they walked and walked until they reached a deep, dark place in the woods. "You search over there, and I shall search somewhere else," suggested the stepmother. "After a while we shall meet here to return home."

Snow Bella gathered roots until nearly dark and returned to the place, but the stepmother was not there. She waited and waited, but no one came. Finally Snow Bella began walking. It soon got dark, however, and she was lost. Suddenly she came upon a little hut in the woods, from the window of which shone a wee light. She knocked at the door, and a young man appeared, saying, "Who is there?"

"My name is Snow Bella," said the girl, "and I am lost in the woods. May I come in for the night?"

"Come in," replied the young man. "I live here with two dwarf brothers, who are asleep. We all work in the deep woods. There is a little soup left. Perhaps you are hungry."

"Thank you very much," answered Snow Bella. "It is kind of you to give me something to eat."

After the young man had warmed the soup in a huge black pot, hanging over the fire, Snow Bella sat at the table and ate.

"Tell me about yourself," said the young man.

"I live with my father and my cruel stepmother," began Snow Bella. "I am afraid she has lost me in the woods because she does not want me back home. I really don't know what to do."

"That is too bad," sympathized the young man. "As

I said before, I live here with my two brothers, who are dwarfs. Tomorrow I shall talk to them about you, and perhaps we shall be able to help you. You may sleep on my bed here, near the fire. I am very tired and must say goodnight."

The young man went off to bed on some straw in the next room, while his two brothers were snoring on their tiny feather beds. After Snow Bella finished her soup and piece of black bread, she went to bed, falling fast asleep.

The next morning she was softly awakened by the young man, while the two little dwarfs with dark skin and wrinkles stood nearby. He said, "These are my two brothers, Snow Bella. You may live with us if you wish. While we work in the woods, you can keep house for us. Be careful, though, whom you talk to, because you are very beautiful and harm may befall you."

Now, the wicked stepmother, thinking that Snow Bella was eaten up by wild animals in the forest, did not worry about her anymore. All day long she combed her hair and admired herself before her looking glass. Then one day she heard someone outside, calling out in a sharp voice, "Mirrors to sell, mirrors to sell."

The stepmother went to the window and called out to the vendor, who was a hunched and wrinkled old man, wearing thick glasses over his tiny eyes. "What kind of mirrors have you to sell?" she asked him.

"Little mirrors, my lady, little mirrors that talk when spoken to. Ask a question, and the truth will be answered."

"Give me one," said the wicked stepmother, thinking that this would be a good way to determine the fate of Snow Bella. The stepmother immediately hung the little mirror on her wall, gazed into it, and sang:

Tiny mirror, tiny mirror,
Of this town and all the land,

Tell me, if you can,
Who is everywhere
Most beautiful and fair?
While I look in you,
Answer true, answer true.

The mirror sang back:

Lady, lady in the mirror,
Snow Bella's the name,
Whose beauty's the fame
Here and everywhere.
Most beautiful and fair
As ever maid be,
And at the dwarfs' lives she.

"Ah, Snow Bella is at the dwarfs'!" cried the jealous stepmother. "I must do away with that girl. To think that she is fairer than I!"

The next day, while the angry stepmother was fretting around for a plan to kill Snow Bella, she heard the sharp voice of the vendor again: "Jewelry to sell, jewelry to sell."

"What kind of jewelry have you?" she asked the old man impatiently.

"Ah, the most cunning sort of trinkets, my lady," replied he. "Here is a necklace wrought with tiny darts in the beads. Whoever wears it will die instantly. Very cunning jewelry!"

"Quick, give me the necklace," demanded the stepmother.

The wicked woman set out for the hut of the dwarfs. When she came to the door, the dwarfs were all away at work in the woods. The stepmother threw a hood over her face and rapped at the door.

"I have a pretty, pretty necklace to sell," said the jealous woman to Snow Bella, who came to open a tiny crack in the door.

"I have no money," answered Snow Bella, who was nevertheless attracted by the beautiful necklace. "I cannot buy it."

"Beautiful maiden, open the door a tiny bit more so I can show it to you," wheedled the stepmother.

"I am forbidden to open to strangers," replied Snow Bella.

"Only put your pretty neck out so I can try it on you, to show you how beautifully it fits," coaxed the mean stepmother.

So Snow Bella put her head outside the door, and the stepmother slipped the necklace onto her slender neck. The poor girl instantly fell dead to the floor. The wicked woman went away, laughing to herself with joy and rubbing her hands in satisfaction.

At the end of the day the young man, who had become very fond of Snow Bella and who was as large as an ordinary human being and more handsome than his brothers, came home with the two dwarfs. He saw Snow Bella dead on the floor. With the help of his two brothers he picked her up, brought her to the bed, and began rubbing her hands to try to revive her. His efforts were in vain, though, because the pretty girl was dead, and all the color had left her cheeks.

Finally the older dwarf noticed the necklace around her neck, exclaiming, "This necklace around Snow Bella's neck is something new! She did not wear this before today." He snatched away the necklace, breaking it from her neck and throwing it to the floor.

Soon Snow Bella's color began returning, and she stirred. The young brother and the dwarfs were overjoyed to have her back alive. They all wept as she embraced them.

"Snow Bella," said the older dwarf, "you must be

careful, my lovely child. Tell us, who was it? Tell us if you have enemies."

"It was no one," replied Snow Bella, not wishing to worry the dwarfs.

After the wicked stepmother was home several days, thinking Snow Bella surely dead, she again went to her little mirror on the wall and repeated her song:

Tiny mirror, tiny mirror,
Of this town and all the land,
Tell me, if you can,
Who is everywhere
Most beautiful and fair?
While I look in you,
Answer true, answer true.

The mirror answered:

Lady, lady in the mirror,
Snow Bella's the name,
Whose beauty's the fame
Here and everywhere.
Most beautiful and fair
As ever maid be,
And at the dwarfs' lives she.

"Can it be possible that this wretch of a girl is still alive?" the enraged stepmother asked herself. "I shall kill her forever this time."

While pacing the floor the next day, she heard the same vendor's voice through the window: "Combs to sell, combs to sell."

"Over here with your combs!" cried the woman in exasperation. "Tell me what kind of combs they are."

"My lady, these are round combs set with tiny poisoned jewels," explained the vendor. "This circular comb covers the head and kills the wearer on the spot."

"Give me one quickly," said she.

The next day the stepmother disguised herself as an old, old woman and set out for the hut of the dwarfs. She knocked at the door, which was opened to a crack by Snow Bella, who asked, "What do you want?"

"I am a poor old woman," whined the cunning stepmother. "Please buy a comb; buy a comb from me. You are so beautiful; it will deck your pretty black hair."

"Oh no," replied Snow Bella. "I cannot talk to you."

"It will cost you only a few pennies," said the woman. "Here, put your head out, and I'll try it on you."

"Please do not beg me," continued Snow Bella. "I want to help you, but I don't know you."

"Here, my pretty child, let me slip it into your hair. If you don't like it, you may return it right away."

So again Snow Bella put her head outside the door, and the crafty stepmother pushed the comb into her pretty black tresses. She fell back inside, dead.

When the dwarfs and their brother reached home late that evening, there was no fire, no food, and nothing done. Snow Bella lay dead in a heap on the floor. They picked up her lifeless body and placed it on the bed. The younger of the two dwarfs began to rub her hands and cheeks to try to bring her back to life, but the beautiful girl was cold. The youngest brother lit a lamp.

Noticing the evil comb in her hair, he exclaimed, "That comb! Where does it come from?"

He pulled it from Snow Bella's hair and threw it to the floor. They all rubbed her, bathing her face with warm water. At last she opened her beautiful, large eyes. "Where am I?" asked she.

"You are all right," answered the young man, holding her hand.

"You and your brothers have been so wonderful to me. I know not how to express it," said Snow Bella.

"Snow Bella," warned again the oldest of the three, "you must be careful in the future. You are too beautiful.

It is the fate of some that their beauty brings good fortune and happiness, but your beauty brings you only misfortune and suffering. I fear it is your wicked stepmother. So beware of a woman at the door in the future."

The wicked stepmother reached home again, singing and rejoicing at what she had done to Snow Bella. "How wonderful I feel," said she to herself, "since I am rid of that bad girl. I know now that I am the prettiest in all the land. Yet I think I shall try my little mirror again." So while sitting before the mirror, she sang:

Tiny mirror, tiny mirror,
Of this town and all the land,
Tell me, if you can,
Who is everywhere
Most beautiful and fair?
While I look in you,
Answer true, answer true.

Then replied the little mirror:

Lady, lady in the mirror,
Snow Bella's the name,
Whose beauty's the fame
Here and everywhere.
Most beautiful and fair
As ever maid be,
And at the dwarfs' lives she.

"This is the limit," gasped the cruel woman in a fit of rage. "Kill her I will! Kill her I will! What shall I do to the wretch?"

The next day, while the wicked stepmother was brooding and thinking how to kill Snow Bella, again the vendor called to the window, "Apples to sell, nice red, red apples to sell."

"Bring me your apples, old man," exclaimed the woman. "How are they?"

"Ah, my dear lady," said he, "a single bite into the peeling and one is dead—a most malefic poison. Yet they are crimson red and most sweet to smell."

"Give me one quickly," said she. "I shall see whether this wretch will live to be the fairest of the land."

This time the stepmother disguised herself as a man and set out again for the hut, carrying the apple neatly covered in a basket. She knocked at the hut door.

"What is it?" asked Snow Bella, peeping through the keyhole.

"I have the sweetest and reddest apples on earth," cajoled the stepmother in the voice of a man. "They are very cheap, especially for you, beautiful maiden."

"I cannot let you in for anything on earth," replied Snow Bella, who looked longingly at the crimson fruit.

"Here my child," coaxed the woman. "Try this one. I shall roll it in under the door."

Snow Bella picked up the poisoned apple, and the wicked stepmother at the keyhole watched her bite into it and fall dead to the floor. She went away dancing for joy and sure that Snow Bella was dead forever.

The three brothers soon came home, saw Snow Bella dead upon the floor, picked her up again, and put her on the bed. They did everything they could think of for three days to revive her, but she remained cold and dead. The apple with the piece bitten out of it was lying on the floor, so they knew Snow Bella had been poisoned by it.

At length they built a coffin from the fine wood in the forest. They sat up all night to wake for Snow Bella, their lovely little housekeeper whom they loved so much. The tears streamed from their eyes.

On the next day they dug a grave into the greensward nearby and began carrying the coffin to the grave. But one of them stumbled and tilted the coffin, shaking up

Snow Bella. The jolt shook her so much that the piece of apple she had swallowed came out from her throat into the coffin. Finally she began stirring in the coffin, and one of the dwarfs saw her and told the others about it. "She is alive!" cried he. "Beautiful Snow Bella is alive."

They took her from the coffin and wept again for joy, Snow Bella embracing each in turn around the neck because she had learned to love the dwarfs for their faithful kindness and warm tenderness. She had also learned to love deeply the handsome young brother, who likewise worshipped Snow Bella.

"This must be the end of the wicked stepmother!" shouted the older dwarf. "Let us go kill her."

Now, the stepmother was at home, rejoicing and arranging herself before the mirror, which she addressed again:

Tiny mirror, tiny mirror,
Tell me, if you can,
Who is everywhere
Most beautiful and fair?
While I look in you,
Answer true, answer true.

Then came the mirror's reply:

Lady, lady in the mirror,
Snow Bella's the name,
Whose beauty's the fame
Here and everywhere.
Most beautiful and fair
As ever maid be,
And at the dwarfs' lives she.

"Hateful mirror!" cried the stepmother, taking the mirror from the wall and dashing it to bits on the floor.

Just then, in came the two dwarfs and the youngest brother. With knives and clubs they fell upon the wicked stepmother and killed her on the spot, making an end of the cruelest and vainest woman on earth. The three returned home, announcing the good news to Snow Bella, who became light as a feather for joy because a terrible weight of sorrow and trouble had been lifted from her life.

The young brother of the two dwarfs, who was now more tall and handsome than any prince, declared his love for Snow Bella. The two were married, and they all lived together happily ever after.

Collected by Calvin A. Claudel from Leota Claudel of Avoyelles Parish, Louisiana, edited by Joseph M. Carrière, and published in *Southern Folklore Quarterly* vol. 6, no. 1 (March 1942).

Rushiecoat and the King's Son

A Kentucky mountain version of "Cinderella"

ONCE UPON A TIME THERE WAS AN OLD WOMAN, AND SHE had a daughter who was the ugliest woman in the world. Rushiecoat was her stepdaughter, and she was the prettiest woman in the world.

There was a dance coming off in the land, and the old woman and her ugly daughter began to get ready to go to it. Rushiecoat said, "Let me go with you."

The woman said, "You're a pretty thing to go!" She poured a pint of rice in a peck of ashes and said, "You have that rice picked out of them ashes and dinner sitting on the table in order when we get back!" And they left.

After she and her daughter left, Rushiecoat started picking the rice out of the ashes, and her mother appeared to her and dressed her in the finest clothes and said, "You go ahead to the dance, and be back at eleven o'clock, and I'll have the rice picked out and dinner on the table in order when you come back."

Rushiecoat went on in her fine clothes, and when she got there, the king's son was dancing. She was so pretty that everybody was looking at her, and the king's son danced with her. Her stepmother and stepsister didn't know her, she was so pretty. When it got eleven o'clock, she quit dancing and went home, got back in her old ragged clothes, and found the dinner on the table in order.

Her stepmother and stepsister come in a-talking and said, "Oh, Rushiecoat, you should have been there today. The king's son danced with the most beautiful girl in the world!"

Rushiecoat didn't let on, said, "Well, I tried to get you to let me go, and you wouldn't let me."

The next day they began to get ready to go to the dance again. Rushiecoat asked them to let her go, but her stepmother said, "No, you're too ragged and dirty to go." Then she poured a pint of rice in another peck of ashes and told her to pick the rice out of the ashes and have dinner on the table in order when they got back.

Rushiecoat's mother appeared to her again and said, "You go ahead to the dance, and I'll fix dinner and have it on the table in order. Come back at eleven o'clock."

Rushiecoat went, and they still didn't know who she was. The king's son danced with her and danced, and she waited almost too late to start back. She hurried to get back in time and lost one of her glass slippers. But the king's son found it, and he went around to everybody to see who the shoe fit. Anybody the shoe fit he was going to marry.

He went to the ugly girl's house too to see if it would fit any of them. The ugly girl cut off her toes and heels, trying to get the shoe on, and when Rushiecoat appeared and wanted to try, they pushed her back in a room and wouldn't let her.

Before the king's son could find her, the women worked on a plan to get shed of her any way they could. The stepmother said, "I'll send her to the end of the world to get a bottle of water." She baked her up some old skins and some old burnt bread crusts and started her out.

Rushiecoat went on and went on till dinnertime, and

she sat down to eat. Then along come an old man with a stick in his hand. He said, "Howdy do, Granddaughter."

She said, "Howdy do, Grandpa." Said, "Won't you come and eat some dinner with me?"

So he sat down and eat with her. Then he give her the stick and told her she was going to meet a gang of wild hogs and told her if she would peck the stick against the ground three times, they wouldn't bother her.

She met the hogs and pecked the stick against the ground, and they went the other way. She sat down to eat again, and the old man come along again.

"Howdy do, Granddaughter."

"Howdy do, Grandpa. Won't you come and eat with me?"

He eat with her and told her she was going to meet a gang of wild bears. She went on and met the bears and pecked the stick against the ground three times. They went away and didn't bother her.

She stopped to eat again, and the old man come up again. Said, "Howdy do, Granddaughter."

"Howdy do, Grandpa. Won't you come and eat with me?"

He eat with her and told her she was coming to the gate at the end of the world. He said, "When you come to that gate, you say, 'Open, gate, open wide for this fair lady to pass through to get her a bottle of water.' It will open wide, and you may go through."

She thanked him and went on till she come to the gate. She done what he said, and the gate opened wide enough for her to go through. When she got to the water at the end of the world and let down her bottle, up jumped three bloody heads. They said, "Wash me and dry me and lay me down easy." So she washed them and dried them and laid them down easy, got her water, and started back.

The biggest bloody head said, "What do you wish on that fair lady as she goes back home?"

The second one said, "I wish she smells so good that every door and window will open to smell her."

Then the second head said to the first, "What do you wish on that fair lady as she goes back?"

"I wish she will be ten times prettier going back than she was coming." Then the first head said to the least one, "And what do you wish on the fair lady?"

The least one said, "I wish every time she combs her hair, she will comb a peck of gold off one side and a peck of silver off the other."

When Rushiecoat got home from her long journey, she was tired and dirty. Her stepmother was cross when she give her the bottle of water. Then Rushiecoat said, "Will you comb my hair?"

The stepmother said, "Come along, my daughter, I will comb your hair."

But Rushiecoat said, "I'll just comb it myself."

The stepmother wanted some silver and gold for herself, so she told her ugly daughter she would send her to the end of the world to get a bottle of water. She baked her up some fine cakes for her lunch and started her out.

When dinnertime come, the ugly daughter sat down to eat, and along come an old man with a stick. He said, "Howdy do, Granddaughter."

She said, "You're not my grandpa."

So he went away, and she went on. She met a gang of horses, and they run over her and like to killed her. Then suppertime come along, and up come that old man again.

"Howdy do, Granddaughter."

"You're not my grandpa."

So she went on, and here come a gang of wild hogs—just about eat her up. She went on till breakfast time, and along come the old man a third time.

"Howdy do, Granddaughter."

"You're not my grandpa."

He went away. She met a gang of bears, and they just about destroyed her.

She kept on till she come to the gate. She pulled at it and opened it a little bit. When she started to go through, it come together and like to pinched her to death. But she got through and went on to the water at the end of the world. Got her a bottle of water, and up jumped three bloody heads. They said, "Wash me and dry me and lay me down easy."

She said, "Get away from here. I'm not going to wash your old bloody heads."

So she started on back, and the biggest bloody head said, "I wish when she gets back she stinks so bad that every door and window will be closed to her."

The middle-sized one said, "I wish when she gets back she'll be ten times uglier going than she was coming."

The least one said, "I wish when she gets back home she'll comb a peck of lice off each side of her head."

She went on back home, and when she got there, her mother said, "Come along, my daughter, and let me comb your head." And when the mother started combing it, she combed a peck of lice off each side.

The wedding day had been set, and the king's son come to take the ugly girl to the church to marry her. They hid Rushiecoat out behind the shed, and the ugly girl trimmed her feet again so she could put on the glass slippers. She got on a horse beside the king's son to ride to church.

There was a little bird that flew up in the king's son's face. It said:

Pretty foot, speckled foot
Behind the shed hide;
Ugly foot, speckled foot
By the king's son ride.

The prince said, "Listen. What did that little bird say?"

The ugly girl said, "You needn't pay any mind to its lies."

The bird said it again. The king's son said, "I'm going to see if it is telling a lie."

He went behind the shed and found Rushiecoat hid. He brought her out and jerked the slippers off the ugly girl and saw what a shape her feet were in. When he tried them on Rushiecoat, they just fit. Then Rushiecoat was back in her pretty clothes again. She got up behind the king's son, and they rode off to the church and got married.

As they were coming back home that night, they had to stop at an inn to stay all night. While the prince and Rushiecoat slept, the ugly girl and her mother planned a way to get rid of her. They got a magic pin from a witch in the inn.

The next morning the prince brought out his horse and waited for Rushiecoat to jump up behind him and start off. But the ugly girl stuck that pin in Rushiecoat's dress tail, and she turned into a rabbit and hopped off into the field and was gone.

The king's son began to hunt everywhere for her and spent months and months searching through the fields and woods but never could find her.

Then one day an old man went back in the woods to hunt, and he found a little rabbit house. He went in it. There lay a young baby on a little rabbit bed. The other side of the hut was full of gold and silver. The old man lay down behind the sacks to see what come in to that baby.

In come a rabbit and jerked off its hide. There stood Rushiecoat. She went back and lay down with the baby and called it King's Son. After a while she was asleep.

The man slipped out and went to find the king's son. He found him at the old woman's house and called him out. The ugly girl and her mother didn't want him to go and see what the old man wanted—said the old man was wanting to tell him some lies. The king's son went out anyway, and the old man told him what all he had seen in the woods.

The king's son gathered him two or three men, and they went to the woods and found the rabbit house. Rushiecoat was gone, and they hid till she come in. When she come in, she pulled off her rabbit skin, and the king's son saw it was Rushiecoat. She went and lay down with the baby and called it King's Son.

When she went to sleep, the men slipped in and held her while the king's son burnt that hide. That broke the spell on Rushiecoat, and she was the most beautiful woman in the world again.

Then the prince took her and the baby to the old woman's house, and they run the ugly girl off. Him and Rushiecoat and the King's Son lived happy ever after.

Collected by Gerald Syme from Georgia Williams of Trosper, Kentucky, and published in Leonard Roberts's *Nippy and the Yankee Doodle and other Authentic Folk Tales From the Southern Mountains* (Berea, Ky.: Council of the Southern Mountains, 1958).

Farmer Perdue's Punkins

A Tennessee tall tale about too much of a good thing

FARMER PERDUE AND HIS FAMILY LOVED PUNKINS BETTER than anything. They could eat them cooked and stewed, made into a pie, or even raw. Farmer Perdue had always wanted to raise them, but for some strange reason punkins wouldn't grow on his farm. He would put extra manure and everything on them to try to get them to make themselves.

He heard of a special kind of punkin seed in a far land that would grow anywhere and make punkins large enough to feed five hundred cows night and morning for a year. So he bought enough of that seed to plant all over his corn patch.

Farmer Perdue planted his corn and punkin seed on a hillside that was so steep, he had to prop his children up on it to hoe the corn and the punkin vines. He planted the seeds on Monday, and by Wednesday the punkin leaves were as big as an eight-pound lard-bucket lid. Pretty soon they had grown so big and so fast that he couldn't see the corn. But Old Perdue said he didn't care as long as he got him some punkins.

They grew and grew and kept growing till folks around there began to worry about them big punkins on the hillside and were afraid they would break off the vines, roll down, and destroy their crops. The smallest punkin was about the size of a cellar, and the largest one was about the size of six barns.

Just after the first frost Old Perdue decided he would cut one of the vines 'cause it was about six feet thick, and he had his boys to bring along the crosscut saw. Time they got to the swag right under the punkin with his horse and wagon, the punkin broke off. The horses got scared and started running down the hill. The punkin caught up with them and would have mashed them flat, but it happened to catch them where a cliff had made a hole in the side of the punkin, and they were caught inside: wagon, team, old man, and boy.

The punkin rolled on and on and finally stopped in the level country. They weren't hurt much, but the biggest trouble was getting out of that thing and getting back home. It took the men and horses two weeks to eat their way to the outside of the punkin and four weeks to get back home, it had pulled so far. And the worst part of it was that they started back with some good seed from the punkin but it took them so long to get back, the seed was froze several times and got ruined.

Soon as they got in, Old Perdue sent them out in a swag to start in preparing to gather one of the least punkins, one they thought they could handle. The boy decided to climb up the vine of one and cut the vine loose so the punkin would probably roll over on its side. He hit the stem a few licks, couldn't hardly get any hold, but then his foot slipped, and he staved the ax in the punkin. Before he could get his balance, the ax just oozed on down into the inside of that punkin. He waited ten or fifteen minutes and thought he heard the ax hit the bottom, but he wasn't sure.

Well, all he could do then was to get back down, go to the house for another ax, hew in the side of the punkin, and find Pa's ax before he missed it. He got in all right and looked around for an hour or two. Finally he met a man stumbling around in there, and the first thing the boy asked him was, "Have you seen ary ax in here? I dropped Pa's in here a while ago and got to find it, or he'll whup me good."

The man began to laugh and said, "Why, son, you can't find that ax in here. I've been here three weeks looking for my yoke of steers."

Published in Emma Deane Smith Trent's *East Tennessee's Lore of Yesteryear* (Whitesburg, Tenn.: self-published, 1987).

Gallymanders! Gallymanders!

An Appalachian tale about the consequences of generosity and selfishness

ONE TIME THERE WAS A STINGY OLD WOMAN WHO LIVED all by herself. She was so stingy, she didn't eat nothin' but ash cakes and water. Well, she was gettin' old, and she had to have somebody to help her with the house-work and all, so she sent across the water and hired her a girl.

Now, this girl, she was mean and lazy—worked just enough to get around the old woman. Didn't care how she made up the beds, didn't half wash the dishes, swept the dirt anywhere she could hide it, just messed along, and slut's wool gathered up all over the house.

Now, the old woman had to go to the store one day, and it was a right far piece from where she lived. So she told that girl she was goin', told her what work she wanted done up before she got back. Then she said to her, "While I'm gone, don't ye dare look up the chimney." And she throwed her bonnet on her head and put out.

So that girl peeked out the door and watched till the old woman was good and gone; then she ran right straight to the fireplace, hunkered down on the hearth rock, and looked up the chimney. Saw a big long leather bag up there on the smoke shelf. Took the poke-stick and gouged it down. Grabbed it up and jerked it open. It was full of big silver dollars and twenty-dollar gold pieces. Well, that girl took it and run. Out the door she flew. Ran down the road a piece, then she took out across the pasture field. Came to an old horse standin' out there.

The horse said, "Good girl! Good girl! Please rub my old sore back. Rub it for me, and I'll let ye ride."

"I ain't goin' to dirty my pretty white hands. I'm rich! Got no time to fool with ye." And on she went. Came to an old cow.

The cow said, "Good girl! Good girl! Please milk my old sore bag. Milk me and strip me, and you can have some milk."

"Ain't goin' to dirty my pretty white hands. Got no time to fool with such as you. I'm rich now." She went right on. Came to a peach tree.

The peach tree said, "Good girl! Good girl! Please pull off these sprouts so they won't choke me so bad. Just prune me a little, and you can eat some of my peaches."

"Ain't goin' to do it! But I'm goin' to eat me some peaches anyhow." And she climbed up in the peach tree and commenced to eatin' off all the good ripe peaches. Eat so many she got sleepy and went off to sleep, sittin' up there in the forks of that tree.

Well, the old woman got back late that evenin', went in the house, and hollered for that girl. When nobody answered, she jumped over and looked up the chimney and saw that her moneybag was gone. She throwed up her hands and run around just a-squallin'. Took out the door and run around the house till she saw which-a-way that girl's tracks went, and down the road she put—a-hollerin' every breath:

Gallymanders! Gallymanders!
All my gold and silver's gone!
My great long money purse!

Came to the horse, said:

Seen a little gal go by here
With a jig and a jag
And a long leather bag
And all my gold and silver?

"Yes, ma'am!" said the old horse. "Come on! I'll show ye which-a-way she went." So the horse and the old woman went gallopin' off across that pasture field, the old woman's skirts just a-floppin'. Came to the fence, and the old woman scooted under it, and on she went.

Gallymanders! Gallymanders!
All my gold and silver's gone!
My great long money purse!

Came to the cow, said:

Seen a little gal go by here
With a jig and a jag
And a long leather bag
And all my gold and silver?

"Yes, ma'am!" said the cow. "She went over yonder. You'll soon catch her." On she run.

Gallymanders! Gallymanders!
All my gold and silver's gone!
My great long money purse!

Came to the peach tree, said:

Seen a little gal go by here
With a jig and a jag
And a long leather bag
And all my gold and silver?

"Yes, ma'am!" said the peach tree. "She's up here right now. You want her?"

"Yes, I want her," said the old woman.

So the peach tree bent over and dropped that girl out—bumped her right flat on the ground. The old woman grabbed her and snatched back that money purse, and then she took hold of that girl and shook her around considerable, and she pulled a switch and switched her legs till she run her off from there. The old woman went on home and hid her moneybag back up the chimney.

Well, the old woman stayed by herself a right long time, but she couldn't get her work done up, so she finally sent over the ocean again and hired her another girl. Now, this girl was all right: a good hand to work. Helped the old woman right well. She never let a shred of slut's wool gather up anywhere in the house.

But the old woman treated her awful mean. Wouldn't let her have a thing to eat hardly, kept pilin' more and more work on her. The girl done the best she could, never said nothin', just worked right on.

It wasn't long till the old lady had to go out to the store again. Called that girl, told her what all to do 'fore she got back, said, "While I'm gone, don't ye dare look up the chimney. Ye hear?" And off she went.

Well, that girl went on about her work: milked the cow and fed the pig and the chickens, washed the dishes and scoured the pots, swept all the floors and made up the beds, scrubbed the kitchen floor, dusted, straightened up everything, swept the yard, churned, hoed the garden, split firewood and carried it in—and then she was done.

So she got out her knittin' and sat down in front of the fireplace. She tried awful hard not to think about looking up the chimney, but she just couldn't keep it off her mind. She stopped her knittin' after a while, bent over—then she pushed back in her chair and commenced to knittin' and rockin' again.

"Ain't goin' to do it! I ain't goin' to do it!"

Then she got tired of knittin'—let her knittin' rest in her lap and stopped rockin'. "Now, what in this world do you reckon she's got hid up that chimney? No, I ain't goin' to look. Ain't goin' to do it! Ain't goin' to do it!" Took up her knittin' and rocked some more.

Well, directly she couldn't stand it no longer. "No harm in just lookin'," she said. So she stooped down and looked right square up the chimney.

"Well, what in the world is that old thing?" she said. Took the poke-stick and gouged it down. Opened it up, and she dumped all that gold and silver out on the floor.

"My! Ain't that pretty!" she said. And she got down on the floor and played with all them silver dollars and twenty-dollar gold pieces awhile. She piled 'em up, made little pens and fences, till finally she got tired of playin'. So she put all the money back in the moneybag and tried to put it back up the chimney, but it wouldn't go. She tried, and she tried, but ever' time it'd fall back down. Got the shovel in one hand and the poker in the other—push it up again, and down it come. So she gave up and just left it layin' there in the ashes. Then she got to studyin' about the old woman findin' it out on her, and she got so scared, she left there a-runnin'.

Got down the road a piece, decided she'd take out across the fields so's not to take any chances on meetin' up with that old woman. Came to the horse.

The horse said, "Good girl! Good girl! Please rub my old sore back. They rode me so hard yesterday, made my old back awful sore. You rub it for me, and I'll let ye ride."

"Well, I'm in a hurry, but I reckon I can do that."

So she pulled her a big handful of grass and rubbed the old horse good. Then he took her up on his back and rode her plumb to the end of the field. She jumped off, and on she went. Came to the cow.

The cow said, "Good girl! Good girl! Please rub my old sore bag. They never milked me this mornin', and my old bag's a-hurtin' me so bad. Milk me, and you can have some to drink."

"Well, I'm sort of in a hurry, but I reckon I can do that much for ye."

So she milked the old cow into a little shiny bucket that was there by the fence. Stripped the cow good and dry. Had her a drink of milk, and on she went. Came to the peach tree.

The peach tree said, "Good girl! Good girl! Please pull off these sprouts. They're chokin' me so bad. You prune me a little, and you can have some of my peaches."

"Well, now, I really oughtn't to stop, but I reckon I can do it for ye."

So she broke off all the sprouts. Then the peach tree said to her, "Now, you climb on up here, and get all the ripe peaches you want. If that old woman comes by here, don't you worry none. I'll handle her."

That girl hadn't had nothin' to eat but ash cakes and water for I don't know how long, and them peaches looked awful good. So she climbed on up to where she could sit easy-like in the forks of the tree, pulled her off a ripe peach, and commenced to eatin'.

Well, the old woman got back, run in the house, and hollered for that girl. The girl never answered, so the old woman run quick and looked up the chimney. Throwed back her hands and commenced to slappin' her skirts and hollerin' and runnin' all around inside the house and out, a-lookin' for that girl's tracks. Saw which way she left and put out from there a-squallin':

Gallymanders! Gallymanders!
All my gold and silver's gone!
My great long money purse!

Traced the girl to where the old horse was at—

Seen a little gal go by here
With a jig and a jag
And a long leather bag
And all my gold and silver?

"Ma'am?" said the old horse, and the old woman had to say it all over again.

"No'm," said the horse. "Hain't seen a soul for quite a spell."

So on she run—flippity-flop!—and she was commencin' to get out of breath.

Gallymanders! Gallymanders!
All my gold and silver's gone! (a-heh!)
My great long money purse!

Came to the cow—

Seen a little gal go by here
With a jig and a jag (heh!)
And a long leather bag (heh!)
And all my gold and silver?

"Well, now, ma'am," said the cow, "I been right here all evenin', and I ain't seen hardly nobody go by here. I ain't seen hardly nobody go by here at all, ma'am."

So the old woman run right on, and she was a-givin' out at every step—

Gallymanders! Gallymanders! (heh!)
All my gold and silver's gone! (a-heh!)
My great long money purse! (a-heh-a-heh-a-heh!)

Came to the peach tree—

Seen a little gal (heh!)
Go by here (heh!)
With a jig and a jag
And a long leather bag (a-heh-a-heh!)
And all my gold and silver (a-heh-a-heh-a-heh!)?

"No ma'am," said the peach tree. "She didn't go by here."

So the old woman went right on—a-loopity-loop!—with her skirts a-draggin' and her tongue hangin' out and her a-pantin' ever' breath like an old hound dog:

Gallymanders! Gallymanders!
(A-heh-a-heh-a-heh!)
All my gold and silver's gone!
(A-heh-a-heh-a-heh!)
My great long money purse!
(A—heh—a—heh—a—heh—a—heh!)

Ran till she give plumb out. Man came along and found her beside the road where she'd give out at, put her in his dump truck where he'd been haulin' gravel, took her on back to her house, and dumped her out by the gate.

They say she never did try to hire no more girls after that. But I never did hear it told whether she finally looked in the ashes and found her old money purse or not. Anyhow, last time I was down there, she was still so stingy she wouldn't eat nothin' but ash cakes and water.

Collected by Richard Chase from R. M. Ward, Ben Hicks, Sarah Hicks, Nora Hicks, and Anna Presnell of Watauga County, North Carolina, and from Cora Clark Mosby and Alica Irvine Clark of Lynchburg, Virginia, and published in Chase's *Grandfather Tales* (Boston: Houghton Mifflin, 1948 and 1976).

The Talking Eggs

A Louisiana tale about two young girls who get what's coming to them

THERE WAS ONCE A LADY WHO HAD TWO DAUGHTERS, and they were called Rose and Blanche. Rose was bad, and Blanche was good, but the mother liked Rose better, although she was bad, because she was her very picture. She would compel Blanche to do all the work while Rose was seated in her rocking chair.

One day she sent Blanche to the well to get some water in a bucket. When Blanche arrived at the well, she saw an old woman, who said to her, "Pray, my little one, give me some water; I am very thirsty."

"Yes, aunt," said Blanche, "here is some water." And Blanche rinsed her bucket and gave her good fresh water to drink.

"Thank you, my child, you are a good girl," said the old woman. "God will bless you."

A few days later the mother was so bad to Blanche that she ran away into the woods. She cried and knew not where to go, yet she was afraid to return home. She saw the same old woman, who was walking in front of her.

"Ah, my child, why are you crying? What hurts you?"

"Ah, aunt, Mama has beaten me, and I am afraid to return to the cabin."

"Well, my child," the old woman said, "come with me. I will give you supper and a bed, but you must promise me not to laugh at anything that you will see."

She took Blanche's hand, and they began to walk in the woods. As they advanced, bushes of thorns opened before them and closed behind their backs. A little farther on, Blanche saw two axes, which were fighting. She found that very strange, but she said nothing. They walked farther, and behold! it was two arms that were fighting; a little farther, two legs. At last she saw two heads that were fighting and that said, "Blanche, good morning, my child; God will help you."

At last they arrived at the cabin of the old woman, who said to Blanche, "Make some fire, my child, to cook the supper." And the old woman sat down near the fireplace and took off her head. She placed it on her knees and began to delouse herself. Blanche found that very strange. She was afraid, but she said nothing. Then the old woman put her head back in its place and gave the girl a large bone to put on the fire for supper. Blanche put the bone in the pot. Lo! in a moment the pot was full of good meat.

She gave Blanche a grain of rice to pound with the pestle, and thereupon the mortar became full of rice. After they had taken their supper, the old woman said to Blanche, "Pray, my child, scratch my back." Blanche scratched her back, but her hand was all cut because the old woman's back was covered with broken glass. When she saw that Blanche's hand was bleeding, she simply blew on it, and the hand was cured.

When Blanche got up the next morning, the old woman said to her, "You must go home now, but as you are a good girl, I want to make you a present of the talking eggs. Go to the chicken house. All the eggs that say, 'Take me,' you must take; all those that say, 'Do not take me,' you must not take. When you come to the road, throw the eggs behind your back to break them."

Blanche walked, she broke the eggs, and many pretty things came out of them: now diamonds, now gold, a fine carriage, and beautiful dresses. When she arrived at her mother's, she had so many wonderful things that the house was full of them. Therefore her mother was very glad to see her.

The next day, the mother said to Rose, "You must go to the woods to look for this same old woman; you must have fine dresses like Blanche."

Rose went to the woods, and she met the old woman, who told her to come to her cabin. But when she saw the axes, the arms, the legs, the heads all fighting and the old woman taking off her head to delouse herself, she began to laugh and to ridicule everything she saw. Therefore the old woman said, "Ah, my child, you are not a good girl; God will punish you."

The next day she said to Rose, "I don't want to send you back with nothing. Go to the chicken house, and take the eggs that say, 'Do not take me.' "

Rose went to the chicken house. All the eggs began to say, "Take me," "Don't take me," "Take me," "Don't take me." Rose was so bad that she said, "Ah, yes, you say, 'Don't take me,' but you are precisely the ones I want." She took all the eggs that said, "Don't take me," and she went away with them.

As she walked, she broke the eggs, and out came a quantity of snakes, toads, and frogs, which began to run after her. There was even a quantity of whips, which whipped her. Rose ran and shrieked. She arrived at her mother's so tired that she was not able to speak. When her mother saw all the beasts and the whips that were chasing her, she was so angry that she sent her away like a dog and told her to go live in the woods.

Collected by Alcée Fortier and published in *The Journal of American Folklore*, vol. 1, no. 2 (July–September 1888).

A Whale of a Hunt

An Appalachian yarn about a mighty resourceful hunter

ONE COLD DECEMBER MORNING ME AND MY PAP WAS standing in our back yard, looking at rabbit tracks in the snow. Pap looked at me and said, "Son, at the end of them tracks is your breakfast."

So I got my old single-barrel shotgun and the only two shells I had and started my hunt. After follering them tracks around the hill a piece, I stopped to rest. Just then I heard a fluttering sound above me, and I looked up and seen nine wild turkeys lit on a tree limb in a big sweet gum.

Well, I knowed I had just two shells, so I decided to try 'em a shot and fired away. I was so close that the charge of shot split the tree limb, and the turkeys caught their toes in the crack. There I had all nine of 'em, and I began to wonder how to get 'em all, but by that time they had beat each other to death flopping their wings. All I had to do was climb up and jerk 'em out of the crack.

Now I had nine turkeys and one shell left, but no rabbit, so I went on a-hunting. The tracks led me down the hill, and I stepped along after them pretty rapid. As I was sliding down through the snow, I heard a loud growling and roaring behind me. I turned around, and there come a big grizzly bear and a wild boar tumbling down the slope, fighting for dear life.

Well, I knowed I didn't have a chance with the gun and only one shell—couldn't kill a big animal with it anyway. So I decided to tackle 'em one at a time. The bear come at me first, and I throwed my gun down and belted my hand right at his old red open mouth. As he come on, I just run my hand right on down his mouth and out the other end, grabbed that bear's tail, and turned him inside out.

That old boar turned on me when he saw he didn't have nothing else to fight. He clipped at me from behind with tushes about six inches long until I got tired and was about to give up as a goner. I jumped behind a little old tree there about five inches through at the butt, and that boar lammed at me and run one of his tushes through the tree. I grabbed me up a rock and bradded the tush on the other side. Had me two flavors of big game and went on hunting for that rabbit.

I follered the tracks down to the creek bank and began to look where my rabbit had holed. As I cast my eye up the creek, I saw nine wild ducks flying down at me right close together. Hadn't more than time to think once about how to get 'em when I cast my eye down the branch and saw nine wild geese sailing upriver. I had only that one shell and didn't know what to shoot at.

Just then I heard a buzzing sound behind me. I turned around, and there I stood, face to face with a big coiled-up rattlesnake. I sure didn't know what to do by this time, but scared of the danger near at hand, I up with my old gun and fired away at the snake.

I don't know what caused it, but my old gun blowed up. The barrel went up the creek and killed the nine wild geese. The kick of the gun knocked me head over heels into the creek.

I began to paddle out of that cold water and come out on land, and first thing I knowed, I had every pocket full of fish. About that time I saw my rabbit hopping around the creek bank, running from the roar of that gun. As I come out, the weight of them fish in my pockets made a button pop off my overalls and whine away and kill that rabbit I'd been after all this time.

Now my hunt was complete, so I took my wild ducks and wild geese, my rattlesnake, and my rabbit, and I put out for home to skin and fry that rabbit for breakfast.

Collected by Leonard Roberts and published in Roberts's *Old Greasybeard: Tales From the Cumberland Gap* (Detroit: Folklore Associates, 1969).

Old Bluebeard

A Blue Ridge Mountain tale about young Jack and the prettiest girl he ever saw

ONE TIME THERE WAS AN OLD MAN AND WOMAN WHO had three sons—Jack, Will, and Tom. Will was the oldest one, Tom was next, and Jack was the least one. The old woman and the old man died and left Jack, Will, and Tom to look after the place.

They was workin' away over in the field, and each took his turn goin' to get dinner. Tom, the oldest, was first, and he tried to see what a good dinner he could get up. He hung the meat up afore the fire to boil, and he fixed some turnips and some potatoes and fixed everything nice for his brothers, and when it was ready, he went out to blow the horn—they didn't have no dinner bell in them days.

Before he could blow the horn, he saw an old man comin' down the road. His beard was as blue as indigo, his teeth were as long as pipestems, and his thumbs were tucked behind him. The man said, "Have ye anything to eat?"

Will said no 'cause he didn't want the old man to come in and eat up the nice dinner he'd fixed for his brothers. Old Bluebeard said, "Well, I'll see about it!" And he went in and eat up everything Will had cooked up, so Will had to fly around and fix something else for his brothers. He fixed what he could, but he couldn't fix much 'cause he didn't have time. Then he went out and blowed the horn down the holler, and when his brothers come in, they said, "What in the world took you so long to fix up such a shabby dinner?"

And Will said, "Well, I fixed ye up a good dinner, but when I went out to blow for ye to come in, an old man come up the holler with his beard as blue as indigo, his teeth as long as pipestems, and his thumbs tucked behind him, and he walked in and eat up everything I'd fixed. So I had to fly around and fix you something else."

Tom said, "Well, I knowed he wouldn't have eat it all up if I'd been here." Will said, "All right, tomorrow is your day, and we'll see what he does to you."

So the next morning Tom put him on some meat to boil in front of the fire, and when he come in from the new ground, he got him some turnips and potatoes and pumpkin and baked him some bread and fixed him a good dinner. And when he went out to blow the horn, he saw an old man comin' up the holler with his beard as blue as indigo, his teeth as long as pipestems, and his thumbs tucked behind him. The old man said, "Have ye anything to eat?" And Tom said no.

Old Bluebeard said, "Well, we'll see about that." And he went in and eat up everything Tom had fixed except just a little bit of pumpkin. So Tom had to fly around and get up something else for his brothers.

When they come in, Jack said, "Why didn't you keep him from eatin' it up?" Tom said, "Tomorrow is your time to get dinner, and see if you can keep him from it." And Jack said, "Bedad, I will."

So the next day Jack put him some meat to boil in the fireplace and got some turnips and potatoes and fixed 'em, and when he went out to blow the horn for his brothers to come in, Old Bluebeard was a-comin' up the holler. His beard was as blue as indigo, his teeth were as long as pipestems, and his thumbs were tucked behind him.

Jack said, "Now, uncle, you just come in and have something to eat." Old Bluebeard said, "No, I don't want anything."

Jack said, "Yes, but you must come in and have dinner with us." Old Bluebeard said, "No, I don't want to," and he took around the house and down the holler. Jack took out down the holler after him and saw him get down into a den—a hole in the ground—and when the brothers came home and Jack was gone, they thought Old Bluebeard had eat Jack up 'stead of his dinner.

After a while Jack come in, and they said, "Jack, where you been?" Jack said, "I been watchin' Old Bluebeard, watchin' where he went to, and I watched him go down a hole in the ground, and I'm goin' to foller him."

So Jack took a big old bushel basket out and put a strop on it, and him and his brothers went to Old Bluebeard's hole. Will said he was a-goin' down. Jack said, "We'll take turns. Will, go first." So Will climbed in the basket, and they let him down in the hole, and when he shuck the rope, they pulled him up and asked him what he found. Will said, "Well, I went until I saw a house, and then I shuck the rope."

"Oh shaw, Will," said Tom, "what did you shake the rope then for? Why didn't you find out what was in the house?"

Will said, "Well, you go in and find out." Tom said, "All right, I will." So he climbed in the basket and went down till he was on top of the house, and then he shuck the rope, and they pulled him up. When he told 'em he shuck the rope when he was on top of the house, Jack said, "You're nary one no account but me."

So Jack climbed in the basket and went down and saw the house and looked in, and there sat the prettiest woman he ever saw in his life. And Jack said, "Oh!

You're the prettiest woman I ever saw in my life, and you're goin' to be my wife."

"No," she said, "Old Bluebeard will get you. You better get out of here."

"Oh no, he won't," said Jack. "He's a good friend of mine, and I'm goin' to take you up and marry you."

"No," she said, "you wait till you get down to the next house. You won't think nothin' of me when you see her." So Jack put her in the basket and shuck the rope. And when she come out, Will said, "Oh! You're the prettiest woman I ever saw in my life!" and Tom said, "Oh! You're the prettiest woman I ever saw in my life."

Jack went on down to the next house and looked in, and there was an even prettier woman—the other wasn't nothing alongside this one. Jack said, "You're the prettiest woman I ever saw, and you're goin' to be my wife. My brothers can have the other one, but I'm goin' to have you."

She said, "Oh no, Jack, when you go down to the third house, you won't think nothin' of me."

"Yes, I will too," said Jack. "You just get in this basket." So he put her in the basket and shuck the rope. When she come out, Will said, "Oh! You're the prettiest woman I ever saw in my life!" and Tom said, "Oh! You're the prettiest woman I ever saw in my life."

Then Jack went down to the next house, and there was the prettiest woman of all. Jack said, "Oh! You're just the prettiest woman I ever did see, and you're goin' to be my wife. My brothers can have the other two, but you're goin' to be my wife. Come get in this basket." She give Jack a red ribbon and told him to plait it in her hair so he'd know her when she come out, and then she give him a wishin' ring. Jack put the wishin' ring on his finger, plaited the ribbon in her hair, put her in the basket, and shuck the rope.

When the brothers saw her, they stopped talkin' to

the other two and fell in love with her right away. Tom said, "You're goin' to be my wife." Will said, "No, she's goin' to be mine." And they started fightin'.

She said, "I won't have nary one. I'm goin' to marry Jack." They said, "No, you won't, for we'll leave Jack down there." So they pulled up the basket, and they commenced to fight and left Jack down there.

Jack just sat there, and Old Bluebeard come in and walked around, but he didn't give Jack nothin' to eat. After a while Jack turned the ring on his finger, seein' how he'd fell away, and said, "I wish I was in my old corner beside the fire, smokin' my old chunky pipe." And sure enough, there he was, and there was the woman with the red ribbon plaited in her hair. And they got married, and when I left there, they was rich.

Collected by Isabel Gordon Carter from Jane Gentry of Hot Springs, North Carolina, and published in *The Journal of American Folklore*, vol. 38, no. 149, (July–September 1925).

Catafo

A Louisiana version of "Hansel and Gretel"

CATAFO WAS THE ELDEST OF THREE LITTLE BROTHERS. THEY lived with their mother and father in a little cabin right by the woods.

The family was poor and did not have enough to eat, so one night the old wife told her husband to go lose the children far off in the woods, from where they never would return. Catafo heard this and planned to fool his parents and save himself and his two little brothers. He filled his pocket with flour.

So it happened. The following morning the old man called his children early. "Get up, children," called he. "Come walk into the woods with me."

Catafo and his two little brothers followed their father into the woods. He went far with them, and Catafo sowed the flour as they walked.

"Wait for me here," the father finally said, when he thought they had gone far enough. "I shall meet you again later. I am going to go a little ways off there."

But the old man never returned. So Catafo took the trail of the flour and told his little brothers to follow him. They followed the trail until they got out of the woods, and they reached the house not long after their father.

"Look! The children have come back," declared the old woman, all surprised. "You did not lead them off far enough. That's why they found the path to come back."

After he had gone to bed, Catafo heard his mother tell his father he had to go lose the children again in the morning. So Catafo got up softly and filled his pocket with grains of corn this time.

After they were on their way into the woods again the next morning, Catafo sowed these grains of corn along the way. Finally their father told them to wait for him in a place where he thought the children were good and lost. And they were well lost, but Catafo intended to follow the trail of his grains of corn.

Catafo waited for the old man for a time, and when he saw he was not going to return, he told his little brothers to follow him, taking the trail of the corn. He followed it for half a mile, but after that he could no longer find the grain. The birds had eaten the grain, and the boys were good and lost. Catafo did not know what to do. He decided on a direction to take, and he and the two little brothers started out.

When night came upon them, they were more lost than ever. The youngest began to weep, and this troubled Catafo all the more. He wanted to go on, but the youngest said he was tired and afraid in the dark. They continued a little way farther, and Catafo saw a light far off in the woods. He showed this to his little brothers, and it gave them courage. Catafo made up his mind to go spend the night there. He went to knock at the door, and an old woman came out to talk with him. She was surprised to see children there at that hour, and she asked them what they wanted.

"I want a place for us to sleep," answered Catafo. "We are lost and hungry."

"I can do nothing for you all," explained she, "because my husband is a devil and will eat you all when he returns."

But Catafo talked her into giving them food and a

place to sleep. They slept in the same bed with Devil's children. When Devil returned, he smelled fresh meat.

"What's the fresh meat I smell here?" Devil asked his wife.

"It's the beef meat you brought here yesterday," explained she.

"Oh no! It smells better than that," replied Devil. "I won't believe that." And he lifted the mosquito-bar of the bed.

"Ah, three children!" exclaimed he. "Now I am going to have some supper! Let me go sharpen my knife to cut off their heads."

Devil went into the kitchen to fetch his butcher knife. Catafo heard this, and he woke up his little brothers.

"Get up!" he cried to them. "We must leave now." They did not want to get up, but he made them get up anyway. Off they went into the woods again.

When Devil returned to the bedside, he did not notice well what he was doing. He seized his own three little children from the bed, one at a time, cutting off their heads. It was his own children he killed. After he saw his mistake, he was angry to death. He looked for Catafo, but he had already left.

Devil got upon his big mule, Ti-Toup, and he took after them. Catafo was going fast, but Devil was gaining on them. One of the children heard him coming. The mule made 600 steps at a time. Devil would shout, "Six hundred steps, Ti-Toup! Six hundred steps, Ti-Toup!"

Catafo saw that they soon would be caught, so he and his two brothers climbed a tree. When Devil got there, he saw them in the tree and stopped.

"Now I will get you all!" called Devil. "I have a big sack under you, and if you look down, you'll fall into it."

"You can wait, if you want," called back Catafo, "but we'll never look down into your sack."

"I am not so sure about that," answered Devil.

Devil sat under the tree, holding his sack open, as he looked up. He waited there a good little while. When he saw that they would not look down, he got up and began to sing and dance. The youngest looked down and fell into the sack.

"That's one!" cried he, tying up the mouth of the sack.

A little while later the second looked down below and fell down as well.

"That's two!" shouted Devil. "The third one isn't far off."

"Oh yes, he's far off," called down Catafo. "You can sing and dance all night, but I will never look down below."

He never did look down either. Devil was getting tired. He told Catafo he would climb up after him if he did not come down.

"Climb if you will," replied Catafo.

Devil climbed the tree. When he got up near the top, Catafo jumped to the ground. He opened the sack, telling Devil that when he looked down, he would fall into the sack himself. So it happened. Devil looked down, and as he fell into the sack, Catafo tied its mouth, having let out his little brothers.

They took a stick and beat Devil until they killed him. Then they turned toward the house again, and Devil's wife was more than surprised to see them alive. Catafo related how they had killed Devil, and she was glad.

"I want you all to come live with me," said she. "I shall be very glad to have you all, because my husband killed my own children."

And that is how Catafo and his little brothers found a home, and they stayed there all their lives, well satisfied.

Collected by Lafayette Jarreau in 1931 from Anéus Guérin of Pointe Coupée Parish, Louisiana, preserved in Jarreau's master's thesis, and later published in *Southern Folklore Quarterly*, vol. 7, no. 4 (December 1943).

Sody Sallyraytus

An Appalachian story about the small and clever defeating the large and strong

ONE TIME THERE WAS AN OLD WOMAN AND AN OLD MAN and a little girl and a little boy—and a pet squirrel sittin' up on the fire board. One day the old woman wanted to bake some biscuits, but she didn't have no sody, so she sent the little boy off to the store for some sody sallyraytus.

The little boy went trottin' on down the road, singin', "Sody, sody, sody sallyraytus!" Trotted across the bridge and on to the store, got the sody sallyraytus, and started trottin' on back.

Got to the bridge and started across, and an old bear stuck his head out from under it, said, "I'll eat you up—you and your sody sallyraytus!" So he swallered the little boy—him and his sody sallyraytus.

The old woman and the old man and the little girl and the pet squirrel waited and waited for the little boy, but he didn't come and didn't come, so finally the old woman sent the little girl after the little boy. She skipped down the road and skipped across the bridge and on to the store, and the storekeeper told her the little boy had already been there and gone. So she started skippin' back, and when she got to the bridge, the old bear stuck his head out.

"I eat a little boy, him and his sody sallyraytus—and I'll eat you too!" So he swallered her down.

The old woman and the old man and the pet squirrel waited and waited, but the little girl didn't come and didn't come, so the old woman sent the old man after the little girl.

He walked on down the road, walked across the bridge—*karump! karump! karump!*—and walked on till he came to the store, and the storekeeper told him the little boy and the little girl had already been there and gone. Said, "They must've stopped somewhere 'side the road to play."

So the old man started walkin' on back. Got to the bridge—"I eat a little boy, him and his sody sallyraytus, and I eat a little girl—and I'll eat you too!" That old bear reached out and grabbed the old man and swallered him.

Well, the old woman and the pet squirrel waited and waited, but the old man didn't come and didn't come. So the old woman struck out, a-hunchety-hunchin' down the road, crossed the bridge, and got to the store. The storekeeper told her, said, "That boy's already done been here and gone—him and the little girl and the old man too."

So the old woman went hunchin' on back—a-hunchety-hunchety-hunch. Got to the bridge—"I eat a little boy, him and his sody sallyraytus, and I eat a little girl, and I eat an old man—and I'll eat you too!" The bear reached out and grabbed her and swallered her up.

Well, the pet squirrel waited and waited and waited, and he went to runnin' back and forth up there on the fire board, and he was gettin' hungrier and hungrier. So finally he jumped down on the table, jumped off on the bench, and jumped to the floor. Went to the store. "Law, yes! They all done already been here and gone. Surely they ain't all done stopped 'side the road to play."

So the pet squirrel stretched his tail out behind him

and frisked out the door. Frisked on over the bridge—"I eat a little boy, him and his sody sallyraytus, and I eat a little girl, and I eat an old man, and I eat an old woman—and I'll eat you too!"

The little pet squirrel stuck his tail straight up in the air and just chittered, but by the time the old bear made for him, he was already scratchin' halfway up a tree. The old bear went clamberin' up to get him. The squirrel got way out on a limb, and the old bear started out the limb after him. The squirrel jumped and caught in the next tree.

"Humpf! If you can make it with your little legs, I know I can make it with my big uns!" And the old bear tried to jump—didn't quite make it. Down he went, and when he hit the ground, he split wide open.

The old woman stepped out, and the old man stepped out, and the little girl jumped out, and the little boy jumped out. And the old woman said, "Where's my sody sallyraytus?"

"Here," said the little boy, and he handed it to her.

So they went on back to the house, and the pet squirrel scooted on ahead of 'em, climbed back up on the fire board and curled his tail over his back and watched the old woman till she took the biscuits out of the oven. She broke him off a chunk and blew on it till it wasn't too hot and handed it up to him. And he took it in his forepaws and turned it over and over and nibbled on it—and when he eat it up, he leaned down and chittered for some more. And he was so hungry, the old woman had to hand him chunks till he'd eat two whole biscuits.

Collected by Richard Chase from Kena Adams of Wise County, Virginia, adapted for retelling, and published in Chase's *Grandfather Tales* (Boston: Houghton Mifflin, 1948 and 1976).

The Peddler's Dream

An Appalachian tale about the power of following a dream

A LONG TIME AGO THERE WAS A PEDDLER. AND BACK IN those days if you wanted to buy something, you would buy it from him. He would carry his big pack to a fair or market where people had gathered, open it up, and show them what he had to sell.

Every once in a while a little boy would come by and pick up a knife and say, "How much is this knife?"

The peddler would say, "It's fifty cents."

When the little boy heard this, his face would fall because that was more money than he had. But when the peddler saw the child's face, he would say, "Take it on, son, and put it in your pocket. It'll be lighter there than it was in the bottom of my pack." And the boy would run off to show his new knife to his friends.

Or sometimes a little girl would come by, and picking up a handful of bright, pretty ribbons, she'd say, "How much are these ribbons?"

The peddler would answer, "They're fifty cents."

When the little girl heard this, her face would fall because her father would never allow her to spend that much money on something he considered plain foolishness. But when the peddler saw her face, he'd say, "Oh, take them on, and wear them in your hair. They'll be prettier in your hair than they ever were in the bottom of my pack." And the girl—maybe she had her eye on some fellow—would tie the ribbons in her hair and run off to see if she could find him.

The grown-ups would just look at each other as the peddler went by, and they'd say, "A fool and his money are soon parted, and that peddler is a fool. He gives away more than he sells."

The peddler lived by himself in a little cabin. Just outside the cabin was a big garden, and in the middle of that garden was an enormous cherry tree. Every night the peddler would watch from his back porch as the raccoons and possums came out of the woods and into the garden to eat his vegetables. Or he'd watch as the mockingbirds swooped down on the cherry tree to pick off the ripe fruit. His neighbors would say, "Why don't you shoo away those thieving birds and animals? They'll rob you blind."

The peddler would say in return, "They don't steal from me. What they take is a payment, for I love to watch the animals at night. They're company for a lonesome man, and there's no place on earth where the mockingbirds sing as sweet as they do in the top of my tree."

Folks would say to the peddler, "You just wait. The day will come when you'll be outside our back door begging for a handout."

Well, little by little the contents of the peddler's pack dwindled down until finally a day came when the peddler had given away everything he owned. That night he went to bed hungry, and a hungry man is bound to dream.

In the middle of the night the peddler thought he saw an angel standing at the foot of his bed, and the angel said, "Peddler, follow the road into town. Stand in front of the courthouse. There you'll see what you're to see and hear what you're to hear." But when the peddler woke up, an empty stomach seemed like a very poor traveling companion, so he didn't go to town.

That night when the peddler fell asleep, the angel appeared again, saying, "Peddler, follow the road to town. Stand in front of the courthouse. There you'll see what you're to see and hear what you're to hear." But when the peddler woke up, he was so weak from hunger that once again he did not go to town.

But that night the peddler dreamed of the angel a third time, and finally the next morning he walked all the way to town, where he stood in front of the courthouse as the angel had instructed. As people went by, he watched them and listened to them, but nobody spoke to him at all.

At the end of the day, as the sun was going down, the peddler, who was now very weak and hungry, wrapped himself in his old coat and began walking toward a lonely alley—to lie down, perhaps to die. He said to himself, "I'll never make it home again. I'm just too weak."

But as he was walking across the courthouse square, an innkeeper came out of his inn across the street. He said, "I've been watching you standing there all day, and not a soul has spoken to you. I want to know what's going on." But when the innkeeper saw how weak and hungry the old peddler was, he said, "Come into the inn and have a meal. If you'll satisfy my curiosity, I'll satisfy your hunger."

So the peddler went into the inn, sat down, and ate a better meal than he had eaten in many a day. When he had finished, the innkeeper pulled up a chair and said, "Now I want to hear your story."

The peddler said, "I dreamed a dream."

"What?"

"I dreamed a dream."

"You mean to tell me that you've been standing out

there in that ice-cold wind in your ragged coat all day long because you dreamed a dream?"

The peddler nodded.

The man said, "I dream dreams too, but I don't pay any attention to the things I dream. I stay here and tend to business like a sensible person. Why, just last night I dreamed that an angel appeared and told me that if I followed the road out into the countryside, I would come to a cabin, and outside the cabin there would be a big garden, and in the middle of the garden an enormous cherry tree. And if I dug underneath the roots of that cherry tree, I would find gold. Where would I be if I paid attention to such foolishness?"

The peddler thanked the man for the meal and walked home, and when he reached his little cabin, he went right to the garden and began to dig under the roots of his enormous cherry tree. Before long he had unearthed an old wooden box, and when he opened the box, he found it filled to overflowing with gold. And the good he did in the spending of it, I haven't the time to tell you.

Told from her family tradition by storyteller Elizabeth Ellis of Dallas—one of many variants also told in cultures and countries throughout the world.

The King's Well

An Appalachian story about the rewards of curiosity

Once upon a time there was three boys who lived with their mom and dad way out in the woods. Their names was Jack, Bill, and Merrywise. Merrywise was the youngest, and they claimed he was the foolishest of the bunch.

Well, Jack and Bill started out one day to seek their fortune, and Merrywise, like he always done, put up a big fuss to go with them. So finally they agreed to take him along and said, "Merrywise, you'll have to mind us, and you can't stop along the road with your foolishness." Said, "You have to stay right with us and act your age."

Merrywise said, "Well, I will." So they fixed their dinner in a poke and started out to seek their fortune. They walked along for about three or four hours, then they sat down to eat out of the poke. Merrywise heard something, so he raised up and said, "Hush, I hear something." They heard a chopping sound way off in the woods up in the mountains. He said, "I believe I'll go up and see what it is."

They said, "Oh no, Merrywise, we've got to hurry. We got no time to fool around with you."

He said, "Well, I want to know what that is. I have to go and see what it is." So he followed the noise and got way up in the woods, and he found an ax up there chopping away by itself—chop, chop, chopping all the trees down. Merrywise caught the ax, took the handle off, put the ax head in his pocket, and come back down the hill.

Jack and Bill said, "Well, what was it, Merrywise?"

He said, "Oh nothing, nothing at all."

They said, "See, we told you we had to hurry, and now we've wasted time waiting for you to fool away time in the woods." So they walked on farther and then sat down to rest. They heard a stream of water like a waterfall, and it kept running and running. So they walked up the hill a piece and found a clear stream of water and got them a drink.

Merrywise said, "I wonder where all this water is coming from?"

"Never mind where it comes from," they said. "Come on and let's go." Merrywise started up the hill again. They said, "Go on, but we can't wait long on you."

He went up into the hills, following the stream until he come to a tiny little walnut. There was a hole in the walnut, and out of it was coming all this water. So he took some moss from the root of a tree and stopped up the hole in the walnut. Then he stuck the walnut in his shirt pocket and come back to his brothers.

They said, "Well, where did it come from?" He wouldn't tell them, just said it come out of a rock up there.

They said, "Now, Merrywise, we're not going to wait on you anymore. We're going to seek our fortune." Merrywise said he wouldn't stop anymore, so they journeyed on and journeyed on for days and days, and finally they come to the king's territory.

And there they saw a big sign, and it said:

ANY MAN WHO CAN DIG A WELL AND FIND WATER FOR THE KING CAN HAVE THE HAND OF THE PRINCESS IN

MARRIAGE. ANY MAN WHO TRIES AND DOES NOT FIND WATER WILL HAVE TO LIE DOWN ON THE CHOPPING BLOCK AND HAVE HIS EARS CHOPPED OFF.

The three travelers hurried on and talked about entering the contest. Bill said he would go first because he was the oldest and strongest. Jack wanted to go first because he could stay at a job the longest. Merrywise said, "Well, I think I'll try too."

They said, "Merrywise, you can't do anything like this."

When they got to the king's house, Bill went on up first and said, "King, I want to enter this contest and try to win your daughter in marriage."

The king said, "All right, but you get your ears cut off if you don't find water. Our whole land is dry, and we want a plentiful well dug."

So Bill took a mattock, and he dug and dug, and he never could find no water. So they laid him down and cut his ears off.

Next came Jack, and he said, "I've got a notion to try this. I can stay at a job longest and dig this well for you."

The king said, "All right, but remember, if you don't, you get your ears chopped off."

So Jack dug and dug, and when he got tired, he just dug right on. But he never did find a thing in the ground but pure old dirt. So they laid him down and cut his ears off.

So Merrywise went up and said, "Well, King, I might as well have my ears cut off as the rest of them. I want to dig your well."

The king said all right, so Merrywise he dug and dug. Pretty soon he was out of sight, so he took his walnut out of his shirt pocket and took the moss out of it and laid it down. He told them to throw down a rope to him, and he come out of there with the water rising and filling up the well. The whole well was full of pretty clear water coming out of that walnut. The king come running out and said, "Well, how did you do that, Merrywise?"

He said, "I guess I just dug in the right place."

The king kept him in the castle that night and never did name his daughter. The next morning Merrywise asked where she was. The king said, "Now, Merrywise, you're a country boy and pretty young to marry right now." Said, "How would you like to have the money of half my kingdom instead of my daughter?"

Merrywise said, "I guess I'd just as soon have the money." So he took the money and went on back home, and he helped his daddy and his mom build a big fine house. His brothers never had come back, so he said, "I believe I'll go and see if I can find them. They had their ears cut off by the king."

They let him go, and he took his ax head in his pocket. When he got to the king's land again, he saw another sign, and it said:

ANY MAN WHO CAN RID THE FOREST OF A GIANT THAT HAS BEEN BOTHERING THE KING SHALL HAVE HIS DAUGHTER IN MARRIAGE.

So Merrywise decided he'd go and look into it. He went in and up to the king and said, "King, what is this contest that you have about getting rid of giants?"

The king said, "Well, this giant comes into my forests and cuts down trees and packs them off for lumber and firewood. If I don't get shet of him, all my timber will be gone, and I won't have any forest left in my country."

So Merrywise said, "I think I'll enter this contest."

The king said, "Well, all right, but they's a penalty. This takes a brave man, and if he don't get shet of the giant, he gets his head chopped off this time."

Merrywise said, "I'll risk it again, King." So he went up into the woods, and he heard a great thrashing and chopping, and he come upon an old giant cutting down trees and stacking them on his shoulder to carry home. He said, "Hey, Mr. Giant!"

The giant said, "Well, what do you want?"

Merrywise said, "I've heard that you're taking all the king's lumber. How many trees can you cut down in a day?"

The giant said, "Oh, a few hundred. Why?"

Merrywise said, "Why, I can cut down more trees than that."

The giant said, "Ho-ho, you little old thing, I know that you can't."

Merrywise said, "Yes, I can."

The giant said, "Well, let's have a contest, and we'll find out if you can beat me. You start over there, and I'll start over here."

Merrywise said all right, and he went over on the other side of the hill and put his ax together and started it chopping. It began to cut down trees right and left, right and left, and when he looked over on the other side, the giant was still chopping on one tree. Pretty soon the giant got tired and said he believed he'd go over and see how the little midget was getting along. He went over there, and there lay half the forest, and Merrywise was standing there wiping the sweat off.

The giant said, "Well, how did you do that?" Said, "You've won, 'cause I've not got ten cut down."

Merrywise said, "Oh, it's easy. I'm just strong and know how to chop."

The giant said, "Well, you're a good feller. Come home with me, and we'll eat supper." Merrywise agreed to go with him, and all the time the giant was thinking about how such a little creature could do all that chopping. "I'll have to take him home with me and see how I can do away with him," the giant told himself.

Then the giant put a big steel band around a bunch of trees and started to load them up on his shoulder.

Merrywise said, "Here, let me help you carry that little load of trees.

The giant said, "Well, okay." He got under the front end, and Merrywise got in the branches and grunted with his end. As the old giant started out, Merrywise climbed up and sat down on a limb and rode out of the forest until they come to this big castle. The giant throwed the trees down, and Merrywise jumped out and said, "Boy, that was a pretty good load for me to lift."

The giant said, "Well, it sure was. I'm tired." They put the trees away and went on in the house. Merrywise said, "After that I sure could stand something to eat, couldn't you?"

The giant said, "Yeah, I think I'll fix me about a hundred chickens and a big tubful of cottage cheese and a tubful of milk and have me a bit of supper."

Merrywise said, "Well, that sounds like a pretty puny supper to me. I can eat more than that."

The giant said, "Come on, then, and we'll see who can eat the most." He set the tubs on the table. Merrywise was sitting beside a window and the giant on the other side. The giant thought he would let Merrywise just about founder himself and go to sleep so he could cut his head off. But Merrywise eat what he wanted, and then he started pitching the food over his shoulder and out the window.

The giant said, "Boy, you sure can eat a lot to be such a little man."

Merrywise said, "Yeah, I know it, but I'm getting sleepy."

The giant put him in one room, and he took the one joining it. Merrywise said to himself, "I know what he's up to, so I'll just get under the bed and wrap up my piller and put it in the bed." He put the piller in his bed and got under the bed. In the night the giant come in the room with a big club with some big nails sticking out of it and just beat and beat on that piller. Merrywise was lying under the bed just a-laughing away. The giant said, "Well, that fixed him," and went back to his room to sleep.

The next morning Merrywise got up and come into the giant's room stretching and yawning and said, "You sure have a lot of flies in your house, old feller. Last night they lit on me and just about worried me to death. I couldn't hardly sleep."

The giant said, "Well," and didn't know what else to say. Directly he said, "Merrywise, you're too big a feller for me. I'm going to another part of the world where they ain't nobody like you." Said, "I can't stay around here 'cause this place ain't big enough for both of us." So the giant picked up a pack, laid it on his back, and left.

Merrywise went back to the king, and he said, "King, I've ridded the forest of the giant and showed you what I could do. I'm not a poor country boy anymore, and I already own as much as half your kingdom. I'm a rich man, and I want your daughter's hand in marriage."

The king said, "I know you are, and I'm proud of you, Merrywise. You shall have my daughter and the rest of my kingdom." So the king moved over and took the old giant's castle, and Merrywise married the daughter and become the new king.

Collected by Leonard Roberts from Jane Muncy of Hyden, Kentucky, and published in Roberts's *Nippy and the Yankee Doodle and Other Authentic Folk Tales From the Southern Mountains* (Berea, Ky.: Council of the Southern Mountains, 1958).

The Walkin' Catfish

A tall Southern Appalachian tale about a boy's unusual pet

I's raised over there at Stoney Point, close to Tucker's Knob. Seem like all I ever done was hoe corn or fish, and I fished as much as I could.

One day I was down there at John Mauk's ol' mill-pond a-fishin', a-catchin' catfish. I's catchin' them fish as fast as I could—pullin' 'em out one right after the other. I was throwin' 'em over there on the bank behind me. After a while they quit bitin', and I commenced to stringin' 'em up. All of 'em had done died and got stiff, lyin' there in the hot sun, except one ol' catfish. He was goin' *whish oo, whish oo, whish oo,* still a-breathin'. Well, I just hung him on my stringin' line and went on to the house.

I started to clean them fish, but I tossed the ol' fish that was still a-breathin' over in the grass. The next mornin' that ol' fish was still a-livin'. You know, I struck up an idea. I just thought I'd start trainin' that ol' fish.

I fixed him up a bucket of water, and I took him out of the water about two hours the first day and about three hours the second day and about four hours the next day, and I kep' on a-workin' with him and a-workin' with him until I left him out all mornin'. Finally I left him out all day long. It wasn't long before that fish had learned to stay out of the water completely and never went near the water at all.

That ol' fish was the finest pet a boy ever had. I named him Homer. I put a little string round him and led him round like a little ol' dog and taught him to follow me. He just wiggled through the gravel and dirt and followed me ever'where I went. Never did I go anywhere unless ol' Homer would go with me. Homer followed me ever'where.

I kep' ol' Homer around all summer long until school took up in the fall. And when I left the house for school each mornin', ol' Homer followed me right on down the road, just a-waggin' in the dirt. I would throw rocks at him to try to get him to go back to the house, but he wouldn't go.

One day as I was walkin' to school, I kep' a-lookin' over my shoulder, and he was still a-wigglin' there in the dirt, a-followin' me down the road. I got almost up to the schoolhouse, and as I crossed a little wooden bridge over a little creek, I looked back, and ol' Homer was nowhere in sight.

I couldn't see him nowhere. I went back there and begun lookin' around that bridge, and there was a board that had broken and rotted and fell off that bridge. I looked down there through that hole, and there ol' Homer lay in the water, drowned.

Told from his family tradition by storyteller Doc McConnell of Rogersville, Tennessee—one of many variants that exist.

Ghosts, Haints, and Chillin' Things

Knock, Knock, Who's There?

A Cajun ghost story about the high cost of greed

AROUND LA VILLE—NEW ORLEANS, THAT IS—THE LAND is so low and wet that the dead have to be buried above the ground in vaults. Folks don't bury the dead in graves in the ground, oh no. If the river were to overflow the levee or a hurricane to flood the land, your loved one might just float back up from the grave and pay you a visit.

Down the river a little ways from La Ville there once lived an old man with his only child, a pretty girl named Thérèse. Her mama had died, leaving Thérèse in the care of her papa, a greedy, miserly man who worked his girl like a mule and dressed her in rags. Although she was of marrying age, he wouldn't allow any young man to court her. She saw no one except her mean old papa.

The only thing he cared for was the gold coins he kept hidden under a loose board in the floor beneath his bed. Every night he would lock his door, and by the light of a flickering candle he would count his golden coins. He loved the way they clinked and glowed and weighed so heavy in his hands.

But poor Thérèse was so lonesome. Every night she would come knocking on his door: *knock, knock.* Her papa would yell, "Who's there?"

"Papa, it's me, Thérèse. Papa, let me in; I'm so lonely. Talk to me."

But her papa would only holler back, "Girl, get out of here, and get back to work. You just want to get your hands on my gold, and that'll be over my dead body."

And so it went, until the night Thérèse fell ill. She rapped on the door as usual: *knock, knock.*

"Who's there?"

"Papa, it's me, Thérèse. I'm sick-sick," she said. "Papa, please let me in."

He yelled back, "You lazy good-for-nothing, get out of here. You're not sick; you just want to get your hands on my money, and that'll be over my dead body."

Again and again Thérèse returned to her papa's door and rapped: *knock, knock.*

"Who's there?" he'd call.

"Papa, it's me. Please let me in—I'm bad sick. I need the healer, Papa; please send for the *traiteur*."

Knock, knock.

"Who's there?"

"Papa, let me in; the pain is worse. Oh, Papa, open the door." But her papa's heart was as cold as his golden coins. At last the girl's cries faded to silence, and she knocked no more.

Then the old man was full of curiosity. But when he opened the door, he found Thérèse lying lifeless on the porch floor.

Now, that old man was too stingy to buy a proper vault for his daughter. Instead he laid Thérèse in a crude wooden coffin and buried her in a shallow, swampy grave down by the cypress tree. The neighbors shook their heads. They warned that there'd be trouble, for how could poor Thérèse rest in peace in such a grave?

Three weeks went by, and a storm began to boil up over the Gulf. The winds churned, and the rain fell like needles as the hurricane passed over the land. Night found that old man sitting in his room, counting his gold coins by the flickering candlelight.

Outside the wind and rain pounded against the

house. The old man didn't know that the river had already spilled over the levee and sent its dark water across the land. He sat in his rocking chair, his lap full of gold, rocking and counting, "One, two, three . . ." Suddenly something thumped up against his porch with a wooden clatter, and he heard a sound at the door: *knock, knock*.

"Who's there?"

Only a great sigh like the wind answered.

"Just a loose shutter," he thought, and he went on counting his shining gold, "One, two, three . . ."

More knocks on his door, stronger this time: *knock, knock*.

"Who's there?"

Only the whining wind answered him.

"It's just that good-for-nothing hound dog trying to get in." And he returned to counting his golden coins, "One, two, three . . ."

At that moment three great booming knocks hammered at his door: *knock, knock, knock*!

"Who's there?"

Only a sad, low moaning.

A shiver ran down the old man's back. "Storm's got me all jumpy. It's just the wind blowing that old live-oak tree, scraping its branches against the house."

But the moaning rose and rose above the howling wind until it became a horrifying scream: "Papa, it's me, Thérèse. Let me in. Papa, let me in. Let me in." And as the eye of the storm passed over the house, a bloodcurdling shriek pierced the deadly calm.

Three days passed, and the waters receded. The neighbors came by to look in on the old man. As they rode onto his land and passed by the cypress tree, they saw that the flood had washed all the dirt away from Thérèse's grave, and it was empty.

They knocked at the back door, but nobody answered. Fearing that some harm had befallen the old man, they went inside. They found him sitting like stone in his rocking chair, cold as marble, his hair gone snow white, with a silent scream frozen on his lips and his glassy eyes bulged out in terror.

Across the room the door hung limp from one hinge as though some monstrous fist had pounded it down. Before it lay a battered, splintered coffin, and inside it was the gruesome corpse of Thérèse. Her withered hands clutched her papa's golden coins, and a ghastly smile was fixed on her decaying lips.

With the money the neighbors bought Thérèse a whitewashed vault and gave her a proper above-ground burial. But there wasn't enough money to buy the old man a vault, so they buried him in a pine coffin down by the cypress tree.

Since that time, whenever the river threatens to flood the land, the old man's troubled spirit rises to warn all that danger is at hand. Folks know he's paid them a visit when they hear *knock, knock, knock* at the door, and nobody is ever there.

Told from her family tradition by storyteller J. J. Reneaux of Comer, Georgia, and published in Reneaux's *Cajun Folktales* (Little Rock, Ark.: August House, 1992).

Old Scratch and the Mean Woman

An Appalachian tale about getting one's just deserts

ONCE THERE WAS A WOMAN WHO WAS MEAN TO HER husband and was always a-whippin' her children and couldn't get along with her neighbors. She was low-down mean. Seems like she just couldn't help it.

When she combed the hair of her little girl, she'd pull her hair and jerk her head nearly off and say, "Hold still!" The little girl would hold as still as she could, but she couldn't hold plumb still. She'd flinch in spite of all she could do, and the mean woman would jerk her hair and pull some of it out and yell, "I'll pull ever' hair outen your head if ye don't sit still!"

She couldn't get along with her husband neither. They never slept near, and she never had a good word for him at the table but stormed at him and said, "I was a plumb fool for ever marryin' ye, and so I was." But the poor man would just put up with her as best he could. And she never had his dinner ready when he came in from the field, tired and hungry.

When he'd say, "Hurry up dinner," she'd yell back at him, "I'm a-doin' the best I can. If ye can't wait, cook dinner y'self!"

She'd knock her little boy down with a stick of stove wood or the poker or anything she could get her hands on. Her whole family was afeared of her, and I don't believe a single one of 'em loved her. I don't see how they could, she was so mean.

Well, one morning that woman got up with a queer feelin'. She washed her face and hands and started to cook her breakfast, but she felt plumb queer. She thought about calling her husband to tell him about her feeling, but she was so stubborn, she just couldn't. That queer feeling kept on though, and it seemed like she was afraid of somethin', she couldn't tell what. She thought something awful was goin' to happen to her. But she went on a-cookin' breakfast and finally got her husband and children up to eat.

After breakfast she got the children off to school, and her husband went to the field to work. That left her there all alone, and that queer feelin' hadn't left her. She felt it all mornin'. Her husband came home to dinner, and she thought about telling him of her queer feelin', but she was too stubborn mean to do it. So he went back to the field, and she went on about her work.

But that feelin' got worse instead of better, and along in the afternoon while she was a-sweepin' the floor, she thought she heard a voice. Sounded like it was up in the chimley. But she couldn't tell, and she wasn't about to look up it to see. Maybe it was only in her mind. So she went on and finished sweepin' and started to get ready to cook supper, when she heard the voice again. This time it sounded like it was behind the kitchen door, and she heard what it said too. That's what scared her sure enough. It said, "Old Scratch is just ten miles away!"

Her hair stood up on her head, and she didn't know what to think. Maybe Old Scratch was a-comin' to get her. She went on about her work, and she wished the children would hurry home from school, but it wasn't time for 'em yet. So she went on about her work, totin' in stove wood, cleanin' the ashes out of the cookstove, anything to keep busy. Then she heard the voice again:

"Old Scratch is just eight miles away." This time the voice seemed to come from down under the kitchen floor.

She was getting really bad scared and thought about calling her husband from the field, but she was too stubborn to let him know she was afraid.

Then she sifted her meal to bake bread for supper and started a fire in the stove. While she was buildin' the fire, she heard the voice again, and it was seemin' to come from up the stovepipe: "Old Scratch is just six miles away." She went on and made up her batter and got the bread in the oven and sliced some meat to fry for supper, and then she heard the voice again. This time it seemed to come down from the roof, right down through the house: "Old Scratch is just four miles away!"

By then it was nearly time for the children to get home from school, and she wished they was there, for she was so scared that she didn't know what to do. Then she decided to go and milk. It was too early, but maybe gettin' away from the house would help, she thought. So she got her bucket and went by the crib and got a few nubbins for her cow and went to milk.

When she got back to her back porch, she heard the voice again: "Old Scratch is just two miles away!" This time the voice seemed to come from the mountain. She looked up the mountain road and could see that the shadows was a-fallin' across the holler. The sun was about to go down.

Oh, how she wished for the children to come home from school. It was time for 'em, she thought. They was always home before sundown.

So she went on and started to get supper on the table, and by the time she was a-doin' this, she was so scared that she was in a weak tremble. And she heard the voice again: "Old Scratch is just one mile away!" She was sure he was a-comin' down the mountain by then, and she expected that maybe he was somewheres up about Sulphur Spring on the side of the mountain.

But she went on about her work and wished to the Lord that she could pray, for she wanted to in the worst way, but she didn't know how. She wanted to 'cause she knowed that her time was a-drawin' nigh. And there was nothin' she could do.

Then she heard the voice again, and it didn't seem to come from nowhere in particular. It come from all around her or inside her: "Old Scratch is just a half-mile away!"

She looked down in the field where her husband was a-workin', and she could seem him unhitchin' his horses to come to the barn. His day's work was done. She looked up toward the mountain, and it was all in shadows. She looked away down the lane, and she could see her children comin' home from school. Her whole body was in a nervous tremble. She was plumb a-scared to death—and if anybody could've been sorry for that woman, this was the time.

She went back into her house and finished gettin' the supper on the table, but all around her seemed to be that voice, not speakin' but ready to speak, and she was expectin' it any minute. How she wished she just had a few more minutes! Time for her husband to get home, time for her children to get home. But her time was about gone.

Then she heard a *clomp, clomp, clomp* on her back porch, and she was so a-scared that her heart was up in her throat. She realized there was somethin' at the door, and it was much darker now in the kitchen. But she was afraid to look around. Her knees gave way under her, and she sunk to the floor, but just as she was a-sinkin' down, she turned, and then she saw him.

There was Old Scratch himself, reachin' his long hairy arms to get her. His long forked tail was a-swingin' back and forth, his peaked ears reached above the top of his head, and his eyes was like flashed fire.

He grabbed her under his arm, wrapped his tail around her, and took off in a lope toward the mountain. The woman was too scared to scream—she was in his power, and she knowed it.

Just as Old Scratch run out of sight with her up the mountain road, she looked back and seen her children again, a-goin' into the yard with their books and dinner pails, and she could see her husband unharnessin' his horses at the barn. But they never did know what become of her.

I reckon Old Scratch took her into a cave up on the mountain or maybe plunged her into the lake of fire and brimstone. Anyway, her husband and children never had to listen to her mean old tongue no more. When Old Scratch gets ye, you're gone for good!

Published in Emma Deane Smith Trent's *East Tennessee's Lore of Yesteryear* (Whitesburg, Tenn.: self-published, 1987).

Spear-finger

A Cherokee tale about the people's battle with a shape-shifting witch

LONG, LONG AGO THERE LIVED IN THE MOUNTAINS A terrible witch whose food was human livers. She could take on any shape she liked, but in her usual form she looked much like a woman. Her body was covered with skin as hard as rock, and on her right hand she had a long, stony forefinger of bone, like an awl or spearhead, with which she could stab anyone to whom she could get near enough. She was called Utlunta, or Spear-finger.

She traveled all over the mountains, around the heads of streams, and in the dark passes of Nantahala, always hungry and always looking for victims. A favorite haunt was the gap on the trail where Chilhowee Mountain comes down to the river.

Sometimes the woman would approach children along the trail near the village where they were playing or picking strawberries. She would coax them, saying, "Come, my children, come to your granny, and let me dress your hair."

When a little girl laid her head on the woman's lap to be petted and combed, Spear-finger gently ran her fingers through the child's hair until she went to sleep. Then she stabbed the child through the heart or the back of the neck with her long awl finger, which she had kept hidden under her robe. Then she took out the child's liver and ate it.

Spear-finger entered a house by taking the appearance of one of the family who had gone out for a short time. She watched for a chance to stab someone with her long finger and take out the liver. She could stab a person without being noticed, and often even the victim did not know it at the time—for it left no wound and caused no pain—but went about his own affairs until he began to feel weak and gradually pined away. He was sure to die, however, because Spear-finger had taken his liver.

When the Cherokees went out in the fall to burn the leaves to get the chestnuts on the ground, according to their custom, they were never safe. Spear-finger was always on the lookout. As soon as she saw the smoke rising, she knew Indians were there and would sneak up to try to surprise one alone. So the people tried to stay together and were cautious about allowing a stranger to approach. If one of them went down to the spring for a drink, the others never knew but that it might be the liver-eater who came back and sat with them.

Sometimes Spear-finger looked like a witch. Once or twice, when far out from the Cherokee settlements, a solitary hunter had seen a woman with a queer-looking hand going through the woods singing to herself:

Liver, I eat it. Su-su-sai.
Liver, I eat it. Su-su-sai.

The song chilled the hunter's blood. He knew he had seen the liver-eater, and he hurried away before she could see him.

At last a great council was held to devise some way to get rid of Spear-finger. The people came from all around. After much talk they decided to trap her in a pit, where all the warriors could attack her. So they dug a deep hole across the trail and covered it with earth and grass to make it look as though the ground had never been disturbed. Then they lit a large fire of brush near the trail and hid in the laurel bushes. They knew Spear-finger would come as soon as she saw the smoke.

Sure enough, they soon saw a woman coming along the trail. She looked like an old woman they knew in the village. She walked slowly, with one hand under her blanket. When she stepped on the pit-covering, she tumbled into the deep hole. Immediately she showed her true nature. Instead of the feeble old woman, she was the terrible Spear-finger, with her stony skin and her sharp awl finger flashing out in every direction, trying to stab someone.

The warriors rushed out to surround the witch. They shot their arrows at her, but the arrows bounced off her stony skin and fell useless in the pit. Spear-finger tried to climb out of the pit to get at the warriors, but they kept out of her way.

They were only wasting their arrows. Then a bird, the titmouse, began to sing from a tree overhead. The warriors thought he was singing *unahu* (heart), meaning that they should aim at the witch's heart. So they shot their arrows where the heart should be, but the arrows only glanced off, with the flint heads broken.

The warriors kept up the fight with the witch without result until another bird, little Tsikilili, the chickadee, flew down from a tree and alighted on the witch's right hand. The men took this as a sign that they must aim there. They were right, for Spear-finger's heart was on the inside of her hand, which she kept doubled in a fist—the awl hand with which she had stabbed so many people.

Now Spear-finger was frightened. She began to rush furiously at her attackers with her long finger and to jump about to dodge the arrows. At last a lucky arrow struck just where the awl joined her wrist, and she fell dead.

Ever since then, Tsikilili, the chickadee, has been known as a truth teller. When a man is away on a journey, if this bird comes and perches near the house and chirps its song, the man's family and friends know he will soon be safely home.

Adapted from the Cherokee Indian tradition by Virginia Pounds Brown and Laurella Owens and published in Brown and Owens's *Southern Indian Myths and Legends* (Birmingham, Ala.: Beechwood Books, 1985).

Wait Till Emmett Comes

An African-American tale about courage and common sense

ONCE UPON A TIME THERE WAS AN OLD BLACK PREACHER who was riding to a church he served at some distance from his home, when night overtook him, and he got lost. As it grew darker and darker, he began to be afraid, but he bolstered up his courage by saying every little while, "The Lord will surely take care of me."

By and by he saw a light, and riding up to it, he discovered that it came from the cabin of another black man. Getting off his horse and tying it to a fence stake, he knocked at the cabin door. When the owner opened it, the old preacher told his trouble and asked to stay all night. The man replied, "Well, Parson, I certainly would like to keep you all night, but my cabin ain't got but one room in it, and I got a wife and ten chilluns. There just ain't a place for you to stay."

The old preacher leaned up against the side of the house and in a woebegone voice said, "Well, I guess the Lord will surely take care of me." Then, slowly untying his horse and getting on him, he started to ride on. But the owner of the cabin stopped him and said, "Parson, you might sleep in the big house. There ain't nobody up there, and the door ain't locked. You can put your hoss in the barn and give him some hay, and then you can walk right in. You'll find a big fireplace in the big room and the wood all laid for the fire. You can just take a match to it and make yourself comfortable." As the old preacher began to disappear into the dark, the other called out, "But, Parson, I didn't tell you that the house is haunted." The old man hesitated for a moment but finally rode away, saying, "Well, I guess the Lord surely will take care of me."

When he arrived at the place, he put his horse in the barn and gave him some hay. Then he moved over to the house, and sure enough, he found it unlocked. In the big room he found a great fireplace with an immense amount of wood all laid and ready to kindle. He touched a match to it and in a few minutes had a big roaring fire. He lit an oil lamp that was on a table, and drawing up a big easy chair, he sat down and began to read his Bible. By and by the fire burnt down, leaving a great heap of red-hot coals.

The old man continued to read his Bible until he was aroused by a sudden noise in one corner of the room. Looking up, he saw a big cat, and it was a black cat too. Slowly stretching himself, the cat walked over to the fire and flung himself into the bed of red-hot coals. Tossing them up with his feet, he rolled over in them. Then, shaking the ashes off himself, he walked over to the old man, sat down to one side of him, near his feet, looked up at him with his fiery green eyes, licked out his long red tongue, lashed his tail, and said, "Wait till Emmett comes."

The old man kept on reading his Bible, when all at once he heard a noise in another corner of the room, and looking up, he saw another black cat, big as a dog. Slowly stretching himself, the second cat walked over to the bed of coals, threw himself into them, tumbled all around, and tossed them with his feet. Then he got up, shook the ashes off himself, walked over to the old man, and sat down near his feet on the opposite side from the first cat. He looked up at the old man with his fiery green eyes, licked out his long red tongue, lashed his tail, and asked the first cat, "Now what shall we do with him?" The first cat answered, "Wait till Emmett comes."

The old man kept on reading his Bible, and in a little while he heard a noise in a third corner of the room, and looking up, he saw a cat black as night and big as a calf. The third cat then got up, stretched himself, walked over to the bed of coals, and threw himself into them. He rolled over and over in them, tossed them with his feet, took some into his mouth, chewed them up, and spat them out again. Then, shaking the ashes off himself, he walked over to the old man and sat down right in front of him. He looked up at the preacher with his fiery green eyes, licked out his long red tongue, lashed his tail, and said to the other cats, "Now what shall we do with him?" They both answered, "Wait till Emmett comes."

The old preacher looked furtively around, slowly folded up his Bible, put it into his pocket, and said, "Well, gentlemen, I certainly is glad to have met up with you this evenin', and I surely am pleased to have yo' company, but when Emmett comes, you tell him I done been here and have done went."

Collected by Isabel Gordon Carter in 1925 from A. Lulu Hill of East Saint Louis, Missouri, and published in *The Journal of American Folklore*, vol. 47, no. 186 (October–December 1934).

Mr. Fox

A chilling Appalachian mystery solved by a brave, quick-witted woman

---

ONE TIME THERE WAS A YOUNG WOMAN NAMED POLLY. They called her Pretty Polly. She wasn't married, and she lived by herself. All her folks were dead.

One day a stranger came into that settlement. Said his name was Fox. Slick-lookin' feller, and he went to courtin' Pretty Polly right off. He'd come to see her of a Saturday night, and they'd talk. Then one day he asked her if she'd meet him the next Saturday night under a big pine out on a ridge there. So she told him she would. But when he left, she got to studyin' about him askin' her to meet him away off like that, and she decided she didn't like it much.

Well, that Saturday night came, and she didn't feel like goin', but she fixed up and went on anyhow. It was cold, and the wind was blowin' something awful when she got out on that ridge. She got to the pine tree, but he wasn't there. She thought first she'd wait, then she thought she'd run back—and before she could make up her mind, she heard him comin' up the holler. Then she thought she'd hide, but there wasn't any place to hide. She happened to look up in that tree, and it had a few low branches to it, so she caught hold on them and climbed right up till she was in the thickest part of that big pine.

She could see down through the branches a little, see what was right under the tree. And directly here came Mr. Fox, carryin' a lantern. She saw him put that lantern on a big rock and sit down to wait. He waited and waited. Then after a right long time he reached over behind a rock, and she saw him lift out a mattock and shovel. He started diggin'. She watched. He kept on diggin', and Polly saw that the place he dug was about six foot long and three foot wide. She kept watchin', and she knew it was a grave and that he was diggin' it for her.

Mr. Fox got the grave started, and then he sat down again. He would look and listen, turn his head this way and that. Then he'd act restless-like—jump in that grave and just dig and dig. He kept on diggin' and waitin' and diggin' till way up in the night.

Pretty Polly nearly froze up there. The wind kept blowin' the top of the tree way over to one side, and the branches would creak and rattle, but she kept holdin' on. And finally she heard a rooster crow way off in the settlements somewhere, so she knew it must be close to midnight. Well, pretty soon after that she saw Mr. Fox pick up his tools and throw 'em across his shoulder, and he picked up his lantern and left. Polly waited till he was good and gone, and then she got down from there in a hurry and struck out for home by all the near cuts she could figure.

Well, Mr. Fox quit comin' to see her after that.

Then it wasn't long till Pretty Polly heard folks talkin' about how three young women had disappeared from around the settlement. Some said Mr. Fox had been courtin' all three of 'em. He'd not come to any of their houses—had met 'em out somewhere. But nobody had evidence of him, so they couldn't do nothin' about it. They'd tried to find out where he lived, but nobody had any notion where his house was at.

Then one day he came to Pretty Polly's place again.

She didn't let on like she knowed a thing, and they got to talkin', and directly he asked her if she'd come with him to his house. She told 'im, "Well, I might sometime."

"Come on and go with me now. It's not far."

"No," she said. "I can't go today."

"Can you come next Saturday?"

"I don't know where you live at."

"I'll come after you."

"No," she said to him. "If I come, I'll come by myself."

Mr. Fox studied about that a minute and said, "If you'll give me a poke of flour, I'll lay you a trail."

Polly got 'im a little sack of flour, and he took it and went on off. He'd sift out a little of that flour every few steps.

Well, Polly didn't go that next Saturday. It was on the next Saturday that she decided what she'd do. She was brave. It hadn't rained nor been very windy that two weeks, so she found the trail all right. She followed it on and on till finally she came to an old rickety house way out in the woods. She hid and watched. Then she saw Mr. Fox come out of the house and go off. And when he was out of sight, she went to the house and went in.

Now, there was a parrot in there, and it talked to her. Polly looked around, and when she went up the stairs and started to open a door, the parrot hollered at her, said:

Don't go in, pretty lady!
You'll lose your heart's blood!

But she opened the door anyhow and looked in. It was like a slaughter room in there: women hung up all around the walls with their heads cut off. Polly shut the door right quick and started runnin' down the stair-steps. Then she heard a racket that sounded like a woman screamin'. She slipped to the window and peeked out, and there came Mr. Fox a-draggin' a woman by the arm.

"Law me! What'll I do now!" Polly asked herself. The parrot told her:

Hide, pretty lady!
Hide! Hide!

"Don't tell him I'm here!"

No, pretty lady!
No! No!

Polly ran and hid under the old rickety stair-steps.

Mr. Fox came in the house, jerkin' that girl along, and he dragged her up the stairs. She reached out and caught the stair rail, a-tryin' to hold back. Mr. Fox took out his sword and hacked her hand off, and it fell through the cracks in the stair-steps, landin' right at Pretty Polly's feet.

Mr. Fox stopped and asked the parrot, "Has anybody been here?"

No, sir!
No! Oh no!

So he pushed the girl in his slaughter room and went in after her and shut the door. Pretty Polly grabbed up that girl's hand, slipped out the door, and ran for her life.

Well, about a week or two after that there was a play-party in the settlement. Everybody went, and when Pretty Polly got there, she saw Mr. Fox in the crowd. All of 'em were havin' a good time, dancin' and playin' kissin' games, first one thing and then another. Way up late in the night they all sat down close to the fireplace where the old folks were, and they got to tellin' tales and tellin' dreams and singin' and askin' riddles.

Pretty Polly slipped out and got that hand and brought it back all wrapped up in a piece of cloth. She sat down again and unwrapped the hand under her apron, where nobody could see. She kept on listenin' to what somebody was tellin'—didn't say a thing. Then directly she said, "I've got a riddle."

"What is it? Tell us!"

So she told 'em:

Riddle to my riddle to my right!
Where was I that Saturday night?
All that time in a lonesome pine,
I was high, and he was low.
The cock did crow, the wind did blow.
The tree did shake, and my heart did ache
To see what a hole that fox did make.

They all tried to guess. Mr. Fox sat right still.

"What's the answer?" they all asked her. "Tell us the answer."

"Not now," she told 'em. "I'll tell you directly." Then she said, "I dreamed me a queer dream the other night. You might like to hear it."

"Ain't nothin' in dreams," said Mr. Fox.

They all begged her to tell her dream, so Polly folded her hands under her apron and told 'em, said, "I dreamed that I went to Mr. Fox's house. He wasn't at home, but I went in to wait for 'im. There was a bird there, and when I went to look in one of the rooms, it told me:

Don't go in, pretty lady!
You'll lose your heart's blood.

"But I cracked the door just a little anyhow, and I saw a lot of dead women in there—hangin' on the walls."

"Not so! Not so!" said Mr. Fox. The young men there all looked at 'im. Pretty Polly kept right on: "Then I dreamed I heard a woman screamin' and cryin', and I looked out, and there came Mr. Fox, a-draggin' a woman after 'im."

"Not so! Not so!" said Mr. Fox. "It couldn't have been me!"

And a couple of the men there moved back against the wall.

"That bird told me to hide, and I ran and hid under the stair-steps. Then I dreamed that girl grabbed hold of the rail, and Mr. Fox took out his sword and hacked her hand off, and it fell through the stairs and landed right where I was."

Mr. Fox jumped up, said:

But it was not so,
And it is not so,
And God forbid it ever should be so!

And several young men moved over between Mr. Fox and the door. Polly paid Mr. Fox no mind.

"Then I dreamed he shoved the girl in his slaughter room and went in and shut the door. And I grabbed up that hand and ran away from there fast."

Mr. Fox hollered out again:

But it was not so,
And it is not so,
And God forbid it ever should be so!

Then Pretty Polly answered 'im back, said:

But it was so!
And it is so!
For here's the very hand to show!

And she took that hand out from under her apron and held it up right in Mr. Fox's face. Then all the men there took hold of Mr. Fox, and they sure did handle him.

After they took Mr. Fox out, everybody recollected Pretty Polly's riddle and asked her about it, and she told 'em about the grave and all.

They took Mr. Fox to town, and they tried him on Pretty Polly's evidence, and he was hung.

Collected and adapted by Richard Chase from tellings by R. M. Ward of Beech Creek, North Carolina, and Polly Johnson of Norton, Virginia, and published in Chase's *American Folk Tales and Songs* (New York: Dover, 1956 and 1971).

Tailypo

An African-American tale about the wisdom of respecting what we don't understand

ONCE UPON A TIME, WAY DOWN IN THE BIG WOODS OF Tennessee, there was a man who lived all by himself. His cabin didn't have but one room in it, and that room was his parlor, his sittin' room, his bedroom, his dinin' room, and his kitchen too. In one end of the room was a great big open fireplace, and that's where the man cooked and ate his supper. One night after he had cooked and had his supper, there creeped in through the cracks of the cabin the curiousest creature that you ever did see, and it had a great big ol' tail.

Just as soon as that man saw that varmint, he reached for his hatchet, and with one lick he cut that thing's tail off. The creature crept out through the cracks of the logs and ran away, and the man, fool-like, took and cooked that tail, he did—and he ate it. Then he went to bed, and after a while he went to sleep.

Well, he hadn't been sleepin' very long when he waked up and heard somethin' climbin' up the side of his cabin. It sounded just like a cat. He could hear it scratch, scratch, scratch, and by and by he heard it say, "Tailypo, tailypo; all I want's my tailypo."

Now, this here man had three dogs: one was called Uno, and one was called Ino, and the other one was called Cumptico-Calico. And when he heard that thing, he called his dogs—*huh! huh! huh!*—and them dogs came boilin' out from under the floor, and they chased that thing way down into the big woods. And the man went back to bed and went to sleep.

Well, way long in the middle of the night, he waked up, and he heard somethin' right above his cabin door, tryin' to get in. He listened, and he could hear it scratch, scratch, scratch, and then he heard it say, "Tailypo, tailypo; all I want's my tailypo." He sat up in bed and called his dogs—*huh! huh! huh!*—and them dogs come bustin' round the corner of the house, and they caught up with that thing at the gate, and they tore the whole fence down, trying to get at it. They chased it away down into the big swamp. So the man went back to bed again and went to sleep.

Way long toward mornin' he waked up, and he heard somethin' down in the big swamp. He listened, and he heard it say, "You know; I know—all I want's my tailypo." That man sat up in bed and called his dogs—*huh! huh! huh!*—and you know, that time them dogs didn't come. That thing had carried 'em way off down in the big swamp and killed 'em or lost 'em. Well, the man went back to bed and went to sleep again.

About dawn he waked up again, and this time he heard somethin' inside his cabin. He listened, and he could hear it scratch, scratch, scratch. And when he looked over to the foot of his bed, he saw two little pointed ears, and in a minute he saw two big round fiery eyes lookin' at him. He wanted to call his dogs, but he was too scared to holler. That thing kept creepin' up until by and by it was right on top of that man, and then it said in a low voice, "Tailypo, tailypo; all I want's my tailypo."

All at once that man got his voice, and he said, "I ain't got yo' tailypo." And that thing said, "Yes, you has," and it jumped on that man and scratched him all to pieces. And some folks say it got its tailypo.

Now there ain't nothin' left of that man's cabin way down in the woods of Tennessee, exceptin' the chimley, and folks who live in the valley say that when the moon shines bright and the wind blows down the valley, you can hear somethin' say "Tailypo . . . " and then die away in the distance.

Collected by John Harrington Cox from Richard Wyche of Washington, D.C., and published in *The Journal of American Folklore,* vol. 47, no. 186 (October–December 1934).

The Hainted House

A Kentucky mountain tale of a wronged man's restless spirit

ONE TIME THERE WAS A MAN TRAVELING, AND HE COME to a place and asked to stay all night. It was an old farmer's place, and he had a lot of work hands. So he told the traveler he couldn't keep him because he didn't have any place for him to sleep. The man said, "Well, who lives across the creek there? Maybe I could stay with them."

"Oh," the farmer said, "can't no one stay there. That place is hainted, and no one has stayed there for ten years." The farmer said, "I can give you your supper and breakfast, but I don't have any bedroom."

So the traveler said, "I'll sleep over there."

The farmer told him, "Well," said, "if you'll sleep over there, why, all right." He said, "What do you want for your supper?"

The traveler said, "I want me a goose to roast."

So the farmer went out and caught him a goose, and the man took the goose and went over to the house. It was a fine big two-story building—looked real well from the outside. So the man went in to stay. Took his goose and built him up a fire and went in to stay all night.

He had his goose in front of the fire and was roasting

it, getting it nice and brown. And all at once a big black cat jumped down out of the chimley. It shook itself and went round and round.

The man said, "Get away from there; you'll nasty my goose."

So the cat went back up the chimley. The man kept on roasting his goose, turning it round and round. A few minutes later a big dog come down the chimley, and it walked round and round the man.

The man said, "Go back; you'll nasty my goose." Well, the dog went away then, and nothing else bothered the man for a while. He eat his goose and sat and warmed himself, and then he got ready to go to bed.

He climbed into a nice bed and lay there awhile, and something started pulling on the cover. It'd pull, and he'd pull. He'd pull, and it'd pull. It was just about to take his whole blanket. So he got out his knife and ripped the blanket in two, and said, "Now, damn you, you take one half, and I'll keep the other'n."

So it took its half and went off and stayed awhile. Then directly it come back and started pulling his other half, and it pulled and pulled and finally took that half away from him. The man said, "I can't stay here without no cover," and he got up and went back to the fire.

He was sitting by the fire when he heard the awfulest noise upstairs—like chains a-dragging over the floor and hammers and lambanging and water a-running and all kinds of noise. He didn't know what to think about it. So he listened to it awhile, and directly he heard the prettiest music he ever heard in his life—fiddling and dancing and singing. He heard it awhile, and he said, "Come down and play and sing for me. I like good music."

He was in a room where the stairway come right down. And the prettiest girls he ever did see and a fiddler come in and played awhile and danced for him. Then he said, "Well, that's all I want to hear of that. You can go back." And they went back upstairs.

He sat there awhile, and directly he heard something else a-coming. He looked toward the stairway, and there come a coffin down the stairs. The coffin scooted on down—there was a chair sitting at the foot of the stairs—and the head of it stopped right in that chair. And there was a hammer a-laying on it.

"Well," he said, "I've seen ever'thing else that's been here tonight. I'll see what's in you." So he went over and picked up the hammer and raised up the lid of that coffin, and in it lay a man with no head on. The traveler said, "I've always heard it said that if you speak to a haint in the name of God, it'd answer you. So in the name of God, I want to know what you're a-doing here."

The man in the coffin said, "Well, I've been here for ten years, and you're the first man I could get to speak to me." Said, "I've got two sons, and I want you to go and call them here." Said, "I was killed here for my money, but the robbers didn't get it. My money is under the hearth rock right here in this room where you are." Said, "I want you to go next Tuesday and have the law come here and my two sons. You tell them what's happened here tonight, that I spoke to you, that I lived here ten years ago, and I own this place. And since then no one's never stayed here. You're the first who's ever stayed all night and the first one I could get to speak to me." Said, "I want you to have a third of my money and my two sons each a third." And he said, "If they dispute what you say on that day, you turn around. I'll be looking over your left shoulder, and I'll tell 'em the same."

So he went and did what the man told him and got the law there. They raised the hearth rock, and there was the money like the man had told him. He and the man's sons divided it up, and that place was never hainted anymore.

Collected by Leonard Roberts and published in Roberts's *Old Greasybeard: Tales From the Cumberland Gap* (Detroit: Folklore Associates, 1969).

Wiley and the Hairy Man

An African-American story about conjuring a conjure man

WILEY'S PAPPY WAS A BAD MAN AND NO-ACCOUNT. He stole watermelons in the dark of the moon, slept while the weeds grew higher than the cotton, robbed a corpse laid out for burying, and, worse than all that, killed three martins and never even chunked at a crow. So everybody thought that when Wiley's pappy died, he wouldn't be able to cross the Jordan because the hairy man would be there waiting for him. That must have been the way it happened, because they never found him after he fell off the ferry boat at Holly's, where the river is quicker than anywhere else. They looked for him a long way downriver and in the still pools between the sandbanks, but they never found Wiley's pappy. But they did hear a big man laughing across the river, and everybody said, "That's the hairy man." So they stopped looking.

"Wiley," his mammy told him, "the hairy man's done got your pappy, and he's gonna get you if you don't look out."

"Yes'm," he said, "I'll look out. I'll take my hound dogs everywhere I go. The hairy man can't stand no hound dog."

Wiley knew that because his mammy had told him.

She knew because she was from the swamps by the Tombigbee River and knew conjure. They don't know conjure on the Alabama like they do on the Tombigbee.

One day Wiley took his ax and went down in the swamp to cut some poles for a hen roost, and his hounds went with him. But they took out after a shoat and ran it so far off, Wiley couldn't even hear them yelp.

"Well," he said, "I hope the hairy man ain't nowhere round here now." He picked up his ax to start cutting poles, but when he looked up, there came the hairy man through the trees, grinning. He was sure ugly, and his grin didn't help much. He was hairy all over. His eyes burnt like fire, and spit drooled all over his big teeth.

"Don't look at me like that," said Wiley, but the hairy man kept coming and grinning, so Wiley threw down his ax and climbed up a big bay tree. He saw that the hairy man didn't have feet like a man but like a cow, and Wiley never had seen a cow up a bay tree.

"What for you done climb up there?" the hairy man asked Wiley when he got to the bottom of the tree.

Wiley climbed nearly to the top of the tree and looked down. Then he climbed plumb to the top.

"How come you climbin' trees?" the hairy man said.

"My mammy done told me to stay 'way from you. What you got in that big croker sack?"

"I ain't got nothing yet."

"Go on 'way from here," said Wiley, hoping the tree would grow some more.

"Ha," said the hairy man and picked up Wiley's ax. He swung it stout, and the chips flew. Wiley grabbed the tree close, rubbed his belly on it, and hollered,

"Fly, chips, fly—back in your same old place."

The chips flew, and the hairy man cussed and damned. Then he swung the ax again, and Wiley knew he'd have to holler fast. They went to it tooth and toenail then, Wiley hollering and the hairy man chopping. Wiley hollered till he was hoarse, and he saw the hairy man was gaining on him.

"I'll come down partway," he said, "if you'll make this bay tree twice as big around."

"I ain't studyin' you," said the hairy man, swinging the ax.

"I bet you can't," said Wiley.

"I ain't gonna try," said the hairy man.

Then they went to it again, Wiley hollering and the hairy man chopping. Wiley had about yelled himself out when he heard his hound dogs yelping way off.

"Hyeaah, dogs, hyeaah," he hollered. "Fly, chips, fly—back in your same old place."

"You ain't got no dogs. I sent that shoat to draw 'em off."

"Hyeaah, dogs," hollered Wiley, and they both heard the hound dogs yelping and coming jam-up. The hairy man looked worried. "Come on down," he said, "and I'll teach you conjure."

"I can learn all the conjure I want from my mammy," Wiley said.

The hairy man cussed some more, but finally he threw the ax down and balled the jack off through the swamp.

When Wiley got home, he told his mammy that the hairy man had almost gotten him, but his dogs had run him off.

"Did he have his sack?"

"Yes'm."

"Next time he comes after you, don't you climb no bay tree."

"I ain't," said Wiley. "They ain't big enough around."

"Don't climb no kind of tree. Just stay on the ground and say, 'Hello, Hairy Man.' You hear me, Wiley?"

"No'm."

"He ain't gonna hurt you, child. You can put the hairy man in the dirt when I tell you how to do him."

"I put him in the dirt, and he puts me in that croker

sack. I ain't puttin' no hairy man in the dirt."

"You just do like I say. You say, 'Hello, Hairy Man.' He says, 'Hello, Wiley.' You say, 'Hairy Man, I done heard you're 'bout the best conjure man round here.' He says, 'I reckon I am.' You say, 'I bet you can't turn yourself into no giraffe.' You keep tellin' him he can't, and he will. Then you say, 'I bet you can't turn yourself into no alligator.' And he will. Then you say, 'Anybody can turn himself into somethin' big as a man, but I bet you can't turn yourself into no possum.' Then he will, and you grab him and throw him in the sack."

"It don't sound just right somehow," said Wiley, "but I will." So he tied up his dogs so they wouldn't scare away the hairy man and went down to the swamp again. He hadn't been there long when he looked up, and there came the hairy man, grinning through the trees, hairy all over and his big teeth showing more than ever. He knew Wiley had come off without his hound dogs. Wiley nearly climbed a tree when he saw the croker sack, but he didn't.

"Hello, Hairy Man," he said.

"Hello, Wiley." He took the sack off his shoulder and started opening it up.

"Hairy Man, I done heard you're 'bout the best conjure man round here."

"I reckon I is."

"I bet you can't turn yourself into no giraffe."

"Shucks, that ain't no trouble," said the hairy man.

"I bet you can't do it."

So the hairy man twisted around and turned himself into a giraffe.

"I bet you can't turn yourself into no alligator," said Wiley.

The giraffe twisted around and turned into an alligator, all the time watching Wiley to see he didn't try to run.

"Anybody can turn himself into somethin' big as a

man," said Wiley. "I bet you can't turn yourself into no possum."

The alligator twisted around and turned into a possum, and Wiley grabbed it and threw it in the sack.

Wiley tied the sack up as tight as he could, and then he threw it in the river. He went home through the swamp, but when he looked up, there came the hairy man, grinning through the trees. Wiley climbed up a bay tree right quick.

"I turned myself into the wind and blew out," said the hairy man. "Wiley, I'm gonna sit right here till you get hungry and fall out of that bay tree. You want me to learn you some more conjure?"

Wiley studied awhile. He studied about the hairy man, and he studied about his hound dogs tied up 'most a mile away.

"Well," he said, "you done some pretty smart tricks. But I bet you can't make things disappear and go where nobody knows."

"Huh, that's what I'm good at. Look at that old bird nest on the limb. Now look. It's done gone."

"How do I know it was there in the first place? I bet you can't make somethin' I know is there disappear."

"Ha-ha!" said the hairy man. "Look at your shirt."

Wiley looked down, and his shirt was gone, but he didn't care because that was just what he wanted the hairy man to do.

"That was just a plain old shirt," he said. "But this rope I got tied around my britches has been conjured. I bet you can't make it disappear."

"Huh, I can make all the rope in this county disappear."

"Ha-ha," said Wiley.

The hairy man looked mad and threw his chest way out. He opened his mouth wide and hollered loud: "From now on, all the rope in this county has done disappeared."

Wiley reared back, holding his britches with one hand and a tree limb with the other. "Hyeaah, dogs," he hollered out, loud enough to be heard more than a mile off.

When Wiley and his dogs got back home, his mammy asked him did he put the hairy man in the sack.

"Yes'm, but he done turned himself into the wind and blew right through that old croker sack."

"That's bad," said his mammy. "But you done fool him twice. If you fool him again, he'll leave you alone. He'll be mighty hard to fool the third time, though."

"We gotta study up a way to fool him, Mammy."

"I'll study up a way directly," she said and sat down by the fire and held her chin between her hands and studied real hard. But Wiley wasn't studying anything except how to keep the hairy man away. He took his hound dogs out and tied one at the back door and one at the front door. Then he crossed a broom and an ax handle over the window and built a fire in the fireplace. Feeling a lot safer, he sat down and helped his mammy study. After a little while his mammy said, "Wiley, go down to the pen, and get that little suckin' pig away from that old sow."

Wiley went down and snatched the sucking pig through the rails and left the sow grunting and heaving in the pen. He took the pig back to his mammy, and she put it in his bed.

"Now, Wiley," she said, "you go on up to the loft and hide."

So he did. Before long he heard the wind howling and the trees shaking, and then his dogs started growling. He looked out through a knothole in the planks and saw the dog at the front door looking down toward the swamps with his hair standing up and his lips drawn back in a snarl. Then an animal as big as a mule with horns on its head ran out of the swamp past the house. The dog jerked and jumped, but he couldn't get loose. Then an animal bigger than a great big dog with a long nose and big teeth ran out of the swamp and growled at the cabin. This time the dog broke loose and took out after the big animal, who ran back down into the swamp. Wiley looked out another chink at the back end of the loft just in time to see his other dog jerk loose and take out after an animal that might've been a possum but wasn't.

"Law-dee," said Wiley. "The hairy man is coming here sure enough."

He didn't have long to wait because soon enough he heard something with feet like a cow scrambling around on the roof. He knew it was the hairy man because he heard him damn and swear when he touched the hot chimney. The hairy man jumped off the roof when he found out there was a fire in the fireplace and came up and knocked on the front door as big as you please.

"Mammy," he hollered, "I done come after your baby."

"You ain't gonna get him," Mammy hollered back.

"Give him here, or I'll set your house on fire with lightnin'."

"I got plenty of sweet milk to put it out with."

"Give him here, or I'll dry up your spring, make your cow go dry, and send a million boll weevils out of the ground to eat up your cotton."

"Hairy Man, you wouldn't do all that. That's mighty mean."

"I'm a mighty mean man. I ain't never seen a man as mean as I am."

"If I give you my baby, will you go on 'way from here and leave everything else alone?"

"I swear that's just what I'll do," said the hairy man. So Mammy opened the door and let him in.

"He's over there in that bed," she said.

The hairy man came in grinning like he was even meaner than he said. Then he walked over to the bed and snatched the covers back. "Hey," he hollered, "there ain't nothin' in this bed but an old suckin' pig."

"I ain't said what kind of a baby I was givin' you, and that suckin' pig sure belonged to me before I gave it to you."

The hairy man raged and yelled. He stomped all over the house, gnashing his teeth. Then he grabbed up the pig and tore out through the swamp, knocking down trees right and left. The next morning the swamp had a wide path like a cyclone had cut through it, with trees torn loose at the roots and lying on the ground. When the hairy man was gone, Wiley came down from the loft.

"Is he gone, Mammy?"

"Yes, child. That old hairy man can't ever hurt you again. We done fool him three times."

Collected by Donald Van de Voort through the Alabama Writers' Project of the Work Projects Administration.

How Things Got to Be the Way They Are

Why the Possum's Tail Is Bare

A wry Cherokee legend about the foolishness of vanity

THE POSSUM USED TO HAVE A LONG, BUSHY TAIL, AND he was so proud of it that he combed it every morning and sang about it at every dance. This went on until the rabbit—who had had no tail since Gator snapped it off—became very jealous and made up his mind to play the possum a trick.

There was to be a great council and dance at which all the animals were to be present. It was the rabbit's business to send out the news, so as he was passing the possum's place, he stopped to ask him if he intended to be there.

The possum said he would come if he could have a special seat, "because I have such a handsome tail that I ought to sit where everybody can see me." The rabbit promised to attend to it and also to send someone to comb and dress the possum's tail for the dance, so the possum was very much pleased and agreed to come.

Then the rabbit went over to the cricket, who is such an expert hair cutter that the Indians called him the barber, and told him to go next morning and dress the possum's tail for the dance that night. He told the cricket just what to do and then went on about some other mischief.

In the morning the cricket went to the possum's house

and said he had come to get him ready for the dance. So the possum stretched himself out and shut his eyes while the cricket combed his tail and wrapped a red string around it to keep it smooth until night. But all the time, while the cricket wound the string around, he was clipping the hair off close to the roots, and the possum never knew it.

When it was night, the possum went to the townhouse where the dance was to be and found the best seat ready for him, just as the rabbit had promised. When it came his turn to dance, he loosened the string from his tail and stepped into the center of the floor. The drummers began to drum, and the possum began to sing, "See my beautiful tail."

Everybody shouted, and he danced around the circle and sang again, "See what a fine color it has." They shouted again, and he danced around another time, singing, "See how it sweeps the ground."

The animals shouted more loudly than ever, and the possum was delighted. He danced around again and sang, "See how fine the fur is." Then everybody laughed so long that the possum wondered what they meant. He looked around the circle of animals, and they were all laughing at him.

Then he looked down at his beautiful tail and saw that there was not a hair left upon it—it was as bare as the tail of a lizard. He was so astonished and ashamed that he could not say a word but rolled over helpless on the ground and grinned as the possum does to this day when taken by surprise.

Collected by James Mooney and published in the *Nineteenth Annual Report of the Bureau of American Ethnology to the Secretary of the Smithsonian Institution 1897–98*, part 1, by J. W. Powell (Washington, D.C.: Government Printing Office, 1900; republished, St. Clair Shores, Mich.: Scholarly Press, 1970).

The Walk-Off People

A humorous African-American story of the Creation

WAY BACK YONDER IN THE BEGINNIN' OF THE WORLD OL' Adam and Miss Eve was livin' on forty acres of good bottomland the Lord had give 'em. They didn't have no boll weevil or high water, and they made a good crop every year. They had 'em two good cows and a heap of shoats and sheep, and they ate their own fryin' chickens because there weren't no preachers there to eat 'em. They had a fine garden full of mustard greens and roastin' ears and a house that didn't never leak. Ol' Adam had the best mules in the country, two brand-new Studebaker wagons, and a pack of fine rabbit dogs.

Miss Eve helped Ol' Adam make the crop. She done the cookin', washin', and ironin', and they got along mighty good. There wasn't but one thing twixt 'em. Ol' Adam was a man who liked to hunt and fish, and ever' time he could sneak off, there he was, chasin' rabbits or lookin' after his trotlines. But that vexed Miss Eve 'cause when Ol' Adam was away, she got kinda lonesome, with no folks around for her to talk to. So one day she said, "Adam, if you don't get some folks for me to talk to whilst you're away, I ain't gonna let you hunt and fish."

Ol' Adam didn't like that 'cause he loved to hunt and

fish more than anything in the world. So he went off down the big road, studyin' what he could do 'bout it, when here come the Lord. The Lord gave Adam hi-dy, and Adam gave the Lord hi-dy.

"Lord," said Ol' Adam, "you sure been good to me. You give me forty acres of good bottomland, and we makes a good crop all the time. You give me Miss Eve, and she sure is a good woman. She helps make the crop and does all the cookin', ironin', and washin'. But, Lord, you knows I'm a man that'd rather hunt and fish than anything in this world, but Miss Eve say if I don't get some folks for her to talk to whilst I'm 'way, she ain't gonna let me hunt and fish. Lord, please, sir, can't you make some folks to keep that woman company?"

The Lord said, "Adam, when do you want them folks made?" and Ol' Adam said, "Please, sir, could you make 'em this evenin'?"

So the Lord got out his almanac—the one with the quarterin's of the moon in it—to see if he had anything to do that evenin', and when he saw he didn't, he told Ol' Adam to meet him toward sundown by the creek that got that good clay bank, and he'd make Miss Eve some folks.

Well, Ol' Adam was right there when the Lord came up on his good saddle horse, got off, and hitched the horse to a little persimmon tree. Adam handed the Lord a heap of clay. He started kneadin' it to make the folks, and Ol' Adam cut some fresh green saplings for the framin' work. The Lord made some Hebrew chillun and some Christian chillun, some white chillun and some colored chillun, some of these and some of those. Then he put 'em all up by the fence rail and said, "Now, Adam, you meet me right here soon after sunup in the mornin'. I'll be back then to put the brains in these folks."

Ol' Adam went back right at daybreak, but it wasn't nothin' there. All them folks had already walked off before the Lord came back, and they've been multiplyin' and replenishin' the earth ever since.

Originally published in David L. Cohn's *Where I Was Born and Raised* (Boston: Houghton Mifflin, 1935, 1947, and 1948).

Luster and the Devil

An African-American account of how Tennessee's Reelfoot Lake came to be

NOW, I HAVEN'T BEEN THERE, BUT I'VE BEEN TOLD THAT the folks livin' out in the swampy lands of Northwest Tennessee are mean. And the meanest swamp dweller who ever lived was a great big feller named Luster. He was so mean that nothing but poison toadstools would grow in his footprints.

Nobody messed with Luster. Folks would keep their distance when they saw him roaming around looking glum, his chin hanging nearly to the ground.

But one time a right friendly feller from East Tennessee happened upon Luster. He didn't know his reputation—and probably wouldn't have minded if he did—so he walked right up to him and said, "What ails you, Luster?"

Ol' Luster was mighty surprised that anybody would ask, so he just said right out, "My foots! I can whip any man that stands, but I can't get my foots warm. I wears sheep's-wool socks summer and winter, but my big ol' foots is always cold as blue spring mud."

"Why don't you warm them at the fire?" asked the mountain man.

"I tried that one time, but it just ain't no use," said Luster. "My foots is so cold that they puts out the fire soon as I gets 'em close enough to do some good. One time I tried shovin' 'em up real fast, and they just froze up that fire till it was nothin' but a hunk of red ice."

The helpful feller from East Tennessee pondered that awhile. "I'll bet it's the damp doin' it. This here old wet swamp is what keeps your feet so cold, Luster. Say, why don't you drain the swamp? You're a big stout feller. If anybody can drain this here swamp, it's you, Luster."

"I'll do 'er!" said Luster. "Gimme a pick and a shovel, man. Yeah! I'm gonna drain this ol' swamp and dry out my foots!"

So Luster got a pick and shovel. He spit on his hands and swung the pick. Ever' time he swung that pick, he loosened about ten feet of dirt. Ever' time he pushed in his shovel and threw out a batch of dirt, it looked like dynamite goin' off.

Luster had worked on it for about a week when one day he quit diggin' and sat down to eat a little somethin'. He was fixin' to take a bite when the strangest-lookin' little feller you ever saw popped up out of the hole Luster had dug and came scootin' up the slope like a rabbit. He was kind of smokin' and covered with soot, and he smelled a lot like a hot iron.

The little man looked real mad. Sparks was just spittin' out of his ears, and little red flames was curlin' out of his nose. "What the devil you think you're doin', Luster?" said he.

"Who wants to know?" said Luster, reachin' for his shovel.

"The devil, that's who!"

"Huh," said Luster. "You look kindly queer, but you don't look like no devil to me."

"Well, I ain't no man. I'm the devil straight from Hell. And Hell's back yard is what you're just about to bust into. I was lyin' out there takin' a nap just now when a clod of dirt hit me smack on the nose. I looked up, and what do I see but the point of your pick stickin' through my roof. Luster, I ain't gonna put up with you makin' the roof of Hell leaky! What with the low grade of coal we got to use, it's hard enough keepin' the fires goin' without lettin' no water in!"

"Just shut yourself up, little man! You ain't no devil!"

"Now, Luster, look at me good. Don't I look like the devil to you?"

"Naw. I know a preacher looks more like the devil than you do."

"Come on now, Luster!" said the devil, gettin' so upset that he begun sweatin' little streams of runnin' fire. "You got to admit I got a tail. Take a look here, Luster."

"Huh," said Luster. "I knowed a man born with a tail and two extry fingers and toes, but he weren't no devil. Come to think of it, I believe he was a Methodist."

The devil stamped his hoof, and fire spouted up. "But I am the simon pure true blue devil, Luster! Cross my heart!"

Luster just laughed. "Prove it. Yeah, prove you're the devil!"

"Now you're talkin' sense," said the devil. "How you want me to prove it?"

Now that's just what smart ol' Luster was waitin' to hear. He said, "Well, my foots is sorta cold, and if you're the devil sure enough, why, supposin' you just go get me a little whiff of hellfire to warm 'em up."

"You got it," said the devil. And he ran back down to Hell and dipped up a pailful of the hottest fire and brought it right back to where Luster was sittin'. Luster took off his shoes and his sheep's-wool socks and stuck out his big ol' feet.

"You sure got a pair on you, Luster," said the devil. "My land! Look at that frost on 'em!"

"Yeah," said Luster, "the minute they hit the air, they frost up like that. Hurry with that hellfire, man!"

So the devil poured some of the fire on Luster's feet.

"Aah!" said Luster. "That sure feels good. I believe

they're gettin' warmish. Pour some more, Brother Devil."

So the devil splashed some more of the pail of fire on Luster's feet. "See there! Didn't I tell you I'm the devil, Luster?"

"You sure did. My, that feels fine! Hit me again." And the devil poured out another dollop.

Just then Luster yelled, "Ouch! You son of a gun, you've blistered my ankle!" And he jumped up and whammed the devil over the head with his shovel. The devil just dropped like a stone. So Luster picked him up and threw him back into the hole and went off on his warm feet.

"These is real foots now!" said Luster to the East Tennessee man, wigglin' his toes in the dirt and grinnin'.

Well, after that Luster was a changed man. The swampers couldn't name a more cheerful, helpful feller. And the next time it rained, that hole Luster had dug filled up with water. The folks wanted to dedicate something to Luster's change of heart, so they called it Reelfoot Lake in his honor.

And if you don't believe me, you can look at a map, or if you like, you can go out there to Northwest Tennessee anytime and see that lake!

Adapted by Marjorie Caldwell of Knoxville, Tennessee, from the story "Luster an de Devil," collected by James R. Aswell in Tennessee through the Tennessee Writers' Project and published in *God Bless the Devil!* (Chapel Hill, N.C.: University of North Carolina Press, 1940).

How Butterflies Got Their Name

A whimsical African-American tale about the earth's beauty

THE LORD HAD JUST FINISHED MAKING THE WORLD, AND he was sitting in his big rocking chair, admiring the work he'd done. But all of a sudden he noticed that something didn't look quite right. This new world was kind of bare. About all there was down there was land, trees, bushes, and lots of water.

So he set about figuring out how to make the world a little nicer. He called one of his angels and said, "Bring me my pruning shears." When the angel brought them, the Lord started pruning all the trees and bushes, and when the trimmings fell on the ground, they turned into the flowers and the grasses.

He noticed that now things were a lot easier on the eyes, and he leaned back in his chair and thought to himself, "Yep, I've made myself a mighty pretty world."

After that he went to take a nap 'cause he was tired. It is mighty hard work making a world, especially when you're the first one to ever think of doing it.

So the Lord took his nap, and when he woke up, he'd hardly gotten his feet out of bed when he heard some talking. He looked down and saw the flowers talking to each other. "It's lonesome down here," he heard them say. "We were put here to keep the ground company and to make things pretty, but it sure is lonesome."

Boy, the Lord was upset. His world was hardly a day old, and he was getting complaints about it already. He had the feeling that he was going to have trouble with the world from now on.

He yelled for one of the angels and said, "Hey, bring me those little tiny sewing scissors." When the angel brought him those little scissors, the Lord bent down and started snipping. He snipped all morning long. All you could hear both in heaven and on earth was the snip, snip, snip of those little bitty scissors. The Lord didn't care what he snipped. He snipped everything—trees, sun, sky . . .

When he finished, he went back to bed 'cause he didn't want to hear any more complaints from anybody about anything. He even thought of staying in bed forever so that the world could handle its own complaints.

Well, there were little snippets and pieces of trimming floating all over the world on the breeze. There were blue ones that had been snipped from the sky, yellow ones snipped from the sun, white ones snipped from the stars, and some that had colors no one could describe.

When the people saw those little snippets fluttering by on the breeze, they called them flutterbys. There were yellow flutterbys, blue flutterbys, and flutterbys of many colors. They flew all over the place.

When the little kids saw the flutterbys and heard what the grown-ups called them, they had to laugh. Wasn't it just like a grown-up to twist his mouth up to say a word? So the kids did the only right thing—they called them butterflies because *butterflies* is easier on the ear and mouth, and that's how a word is supposed to be.

Well, grown-ups heard the kids calling the flutterbys *butterflies* and decided that that word made eminently more sense, so they started calling them butterflies too.

That's how the butterflies came to be and how they got their name. And that's why you always see butterflies around flowers, because they were made to keep the flowers company.

Told by Giles Asbury and published in John Harrell's *A Storyteller's Treasury* (Berkeley, Calif.: York House, 1977).

The Magic Sausage Mill

A Kentucky mountain tale that explains why the seas are salty

I'LL TELL YE ONE ABOUT A RICH BROTHER AND A POOR brother. The rich brother had plenty of ever'thing a man needed. The poor brother didn't have nothing much and worked for his rich brother, just a little every day. For his pay, he'd take meat or about anything he could get.

Well, his rich brother knew about a place nearby where a lot of goblins stayed and a woodcutter who worked around there, cuttin' wood. The rich brother told his poor brother he would have to be awful careful with his meat if he went by there and the goblins were around. He said them goblins would try to take it away from him. Well, the poor brother went by that place, and the old woodcutter asked him what he had, and he told the woodcutter he had meat.

"Well," he said, "if the goblins find it out, they'll take it away from you. But they got a mill, a magic mill that'll grind anything you want it to grind, and it's a-sitting behind the door." Said, "If you'll throw that meat in to 'em, while they're a-fighting over it, you can get that mill. Bring it out, and I'll tell you how to operate it."

Well, so he did. He throwed the meat to the goblins. While they was onto the meat, a-fightin' over it, the poor brother got the mill and come back out to the woodcutter. The woodcutter said, "Now, when you want to grind anything—this mill will grind anything you want—you just tell it what to do. But you have to say, 'Hoky, spoky, foky, stop,' to make it stop."

So the poor brother took the mill, and he went home. His wife met him at the door, thinking he'd have something to eat. He told her that he took meat for his work, but he swapped it on a mill. She stormed at him over takin' that old rusty-looking thing. "Well," he said, "you get ready now, and we'll have us plenty of forks and knives and things to eat with." Said, "We'll have food to eat with 'em too."

He got ready, and he told the mill, "Grind knives and forks." So the mill obeyed him and ground what they wanted of knives and forks. He told it to stop grinding them. Then he told it to bring out plates and teacups and all the things they wanted to eat out of and then cooking vessels. And he told the mill to grind sausage.

So the mill obeyed him and ground them a big meal of sausage, and then he said the magic words to get it to stop: "Hoky, spoky, foky, stop!" Well, he ground all kinds of food and anything else he wanted, and he didn't have to work for his brother anymore.

Pretty soon his brother got kindly uneasy, and he went to see about him because he didn't have to work anymore. The poor brother told him, "I've quit work. I've got a mill now." Said, "I can collect all the things I need without work."

Well, the rich brother insisted on him that he wanted to see some tricks that the mill could do. The poor brother told him to watch, and he'd show him. He got the mill and told it to grind sausage, and it did. But when he stopped it, he spoke the magic words in a low tone so his brother couldn't hear him. His brother said, "Well, can you grind fish with the thing?"

So the poor brother spoke again, and big fish commenced to flopping out, and that surprised the rich brother. Then he ground gravy, and he ground bread, and he ground corn pone—just anything he wanted to eat.

Well, his brother insisted on him to sell that mill. But the poor brother said, "I don't want to."

"Well," the rich brother said, "sell it to me, and you still won't have to work. You let me have the mill." The poor brother finally asked what his brother would give for it.

The rich brother said, "I'll give you two thousand dollars for the mill, and you can come to the house whenever you want anything, and I'll grind whatever you want and need to eat." So the poor brother traded with him.

The rich brother said, "You help me take the mill home and help me start it out till I can operate it, then I'll pay you your money." So the poor brother took the mill over, helped his brother set it up, got his money, and went back to his house.

The rich brother looked the mill over, and then he told his wife, "You go to the field to work tomorrow, and I'll get dinner for us." Said, "I'll have fish and gravy and sausage—just a good old dinner when you come in."

She said, "All right, if you can cook like that, I'll go work." So she went to work.

Now, the poor brother had left the mill with his brother all right, and he told him how to start the mill, but he didn't tell him how to stop it. The rich brother was so anxious to start that he hurried up and got him a pan, and he told the mill to grind fish and gravy and grind it fast.

Well, the mill went to grindin', and the big fish flopped out, and in a minute he had the pan run over. He said, "Stop!" But that wasn't the magic words to stop the mill, and the mill didn't stop. He said again, "Stop!" But the mill didn't stop.

The pan run over, and the fish and gravy was running into the house. Well, he called out, "Stop!" again, and he began to cuss that mill, but it wouldn't stop. He didn't know anything else but to throw the mill out.

So he throwed it out the door, but still the mill kept on grinding. It was grinding out a big old stream of fish and gravy, and the fish went a-floppin' on toward town. The gravy kept on runnin', and the fish kept on floppin', and he saw it was a-goin' to run the town over. So he run back to his poor brother.

The rich brother said, "Brother, I want you to go quick and stop that mill." Said, "It's a-grindin' fish and gravy, and it's a-goin' to flood the town if you don't do something with it."

The poor brother said, "Let's sit down and talk awhile. Take you a chair and sit down, and we'll talk about that mill awhile." Said, "What did you say about that mill?"

His brother said, "Hurry! I'll give you two thousand dollars more if you'll go and stop that mill. Do something with it, and I'll give you that old mill back."

So he got up slowly and went with his brother and got his two thousand dollars that his brother said he'd give him to get that mill and take it away. He stopped the mill and took it on home with him. By then he was wealthy by his rich brother's money. He'd paid him to get the mill and then paid him for takin' the mill off his hands.

Well, there was an old storekeeper near there, and he bought up all sorts of stuff—salt and wheat and such—and took it across the sea from one nation to another to sell it. He'd heard about the poor man having that mill. The rich brother had told the storekeeper that his brother had it and that it would grind anything, in any amount he wanted.

So the storekeeper come to see the poor brother about the mill. He asked him, "What'll you take for that mill?"

"Oh," the poor brother said, "I don't want to sell it. I want to keep it to grind my grub and stuff with."

"Well," the storekeeper said, "I'll give you enough money so you won't have to grind anything. You'll have enough money to buy whatever you want."

The poor brother said, "Well, how much will you give me?"

The man said, "I'll give you ten thousand dollars in cash for that mill."

He said, "Hoky doh, I'll trade you the mill."

So the storekeeper took the mill and put it on his ship, and he got ready to grind. He was aimin' to grind a shipload of salt as he went across the sea and take it to another nation. Well, he started the mill to grinding salt, and he told it to grind its best. The mill started to whirrin', and the salt went to pourin'—filled ever' bag he had plumb full and ever' tub, ever' box too.

The storekeeper said, "Stop!" But the mill wouldn't obey. That wasn't the words to get it to stop, so it just kept on grindin' salt. By that time the salt had got so heavy that it was almost sinkin' the ship, so he throwed the mill out into the sea. And if you don't think that the mill is grindin' today in the sea, you just taste of the sea water and see if it ain't salty.

Collected by Leonard Roberts and published in Roberts's *Sang Branch Settlers: Folksongs and Tales of a Kentucky Mountain Family* (Austin, Texas: University of Texas Press in conjunction with the American Folklore Society, 1974).

Rabbit's Tail

An African-American story about the day the rabbit lost his long tail

THIS STORY HAPPENED A LONG, LONG, LONG, LONG, LONG time ago—back in the days when rabbits had long, beautiful, glossy, bushy tails. In fact, there was one rabbit who thought that he had the very best tail of all. He thought his tail was better than a fox's tail or a squirrel's tail or even a raccoon's tail.

Now, when Rabbit would go hopping through the forest, he'd hop just as high off the ground as he could so as to keep his tail from being dragged through the mud or caught in the bushes and such.

One day he was hopping along just as high and happy as you please, with his tail flowing along behind, the way he liked it.

Bumpty, bumpty, bumpty, bump. Bumpty, bumpty, bumpty, bump!

All of a sudden he came to an oooey, gooey, slimy, sticky, muddy swamp.

"Oooey!" said Rabbit, "I don't wanna go through that swamp! Why, I'll get my feet all messed up and my tail all muddy."

But he did have to get to the other side. So he started looking for a way around that swamp. He looked to the east. It was a *long* way around that way. He looked to the west. It was even longer that way.

It seemed that the only way to go was right through the middle of that swamp. So he started out, putting one foot in to test the situation.

"Oooey!" He moved over where things looked a little more solid, and he tried again.

"Bleh! I ain't going through that swamp, and that's that!" he decided. Still, he did have to get to the other side. So he sat down, and he thought. And he thought. And he thought, and he thought, and he thought, and he thought.

Finally he thought up a plan. He stood up right where he was, on solid ground, and he hollered out, "Alligator!"

Nothing happened.

"Alligator!"

Still nothing.

"I sure do wish I could find Alligator!"

Just then, up out of that slimy mud there came a lumpy, bumpy, green alligator.

"What do you want?"

"Why, I don't want nothing, Alligator. I was just passing by the swamp, and I was thinking about you and how lonely you must be, so I just figured I'd stop and pass the time of day with you. You know, keep you from being so lonely and all," said Rabbit.

"What are you talking about? I am not lonely! I've got plenty of family and friends in this here swamp!"

"Now, Alligator, you don't have to go saying things like that to me 'cause I know they ain't true. Why, every time I come by here, you're all by yourself—just like you are right now—and I just think it's pitiful, that's all. So I came by here to keep you company."

"You ain't listening to me! I'm telling you I got plenty of family and friends in this here swamp. As a matter of fact, I got more family than you do!"

Rabbit nearly fell into the swamp, he was laughing so hard.

"He-he, he-he, he-he, he-he! Everybody knows that rabbits have thousands and thousands and thousands in their families. Just look at you, all by yourself, just like you always are. You shouldn't go saying things you can't prove, Alligator!"

"I can prove it! I can, and I will! You just wait right here." Alligator went swimming off through the swamp. "Here, gator, gator, gator! Here, gator!"

Up from that slimy mud there came dozens and dozens, hundreds and hundreds, thousands and thousands of alligators. Green ones, gray ones, black ones, brown ones—all of them lumpy and bumpy and ugly.

"Oooey!" cried Rabbit, "you sure do have a lot of alligators in your family. Why, that's a nice big family—a family to be proud of. 'Course, it's not as big as my family, but it's a nice-sized family all the same."

Alligator was not pleased with this pronouncement.

"My family's bigger than your family, I tell you! You just count 'em, and see for yourself!"

"You want me to count a-l-l-l these alligators?" cried Rabbit as he looked around the swamp.

"Count 'em!"

"Yessir, I think I will. Let's see . . . one, two, three . . . No! That tail seems to be part of that head, and I already counted that one. I've gotta start again. One, two . . . Oh, Alligator, they keep on movin' around! They keep on slimin' over each other and around each other and gettin' all tangled up with each other! Now, how am I supposed to count 'em if they won't stand still? If you want me to count 'em, you're gonna have to get 'em to stay still—maybe even get 'em to line up.

"Yeah, maybe you can make 'em go in a straight line, say from that end of the swamp over to this end. If they was to line up, I could count 'em. But if they don't, I won't. It's up to you."

"All right, alligators! Line up!"

And the alligators lined up: nose to toes, nose to toes,

nose to toes, all the way across that swamp, in one long, lumpy, bumpy, green and gray and black and brown alligator line. From one end of the swamp a-l-l-l the way to the other end.

"There! Now you can count 'em!" said Rabbit.

"Uh-uh. I ain't countin' 'em. You are. Get to countin'!"

"Oh, all right. If you want me to, I guess I will."

Rabbit hopped onto the first alligator's back. Bumpty!

"One," he said.

He jumped to the next alligator's back. Bumpty!

"Two," he counted.

He jumped to the next alligator's back. Bumpty!

"Three," he said.

He jumped to another alligator's back.

Bumpty, bumpty, bumpty, bump!

"Four, five, six, seven."

Bumpty, bumpty, bumpty, bump!

"Eight, nine, ten, eleven."

He kept on jumping from one alligator to the next and countin' as he went.

Bumpty, bumpty, bumpty, bumpty, bumpty, bumpty, bumpty, bump!

He just kept jumping as high and happy as you please, never once touching his feet to that swamp or even getting his tail in the mud. His tail was just flowing along behind, the way he liked it.

Bumpty, bumpty, bumpty, bumpty, bumpty, bumpty, bumpty, bumpty, bumpty, bump!

Finally he landed on the last alligator's back.

Now, that alligator had been sittin' in that mud for the *longest* time, with his toes stuck in somebody else's nose and his nose buried in the slime of that swamp, and he was not happy with the situation. As a matter of fact, he blamed his situation on Rabbit.

So when Rabbit hopped on his back and sighed, "Two thousand seven hundred and nineteen! Whew, that's a lot of alligators!" and got ready to jump off the alligator's back onto dry land, that alligator was ready.

He opened up his great, big mouth full of sharp, white teeth, and he closed it with a *snap!* that snapped off most of Rabbit's tail.

That's why, from that day to this, rabbits have all had little short fluffy tails.

And that's the end of one rabbit's tale.

Adapted and told by storyteller Sherry Des Enfants of Lithonia, Georgia.

Tricksters and Fools

The Two Old Women's Bet

An Appalachian tale about wives who wager on their husbands' foolishness

ONE TIME THERE WERE TWO OLD WOMEN GOT TO TALKIN' about the menfolks: how foolish they could act and what was the craziest fool thing their husbands had ever done. They got to arguin', so finally they made a bet about which one could make the biggest fool of her husband.

So one of 'em said to her man when he come in from work that evenin', said, "Old man, do you feel all right?"

"Yes," he said, "I feel fine."

"Well," she told him, "you sure do look awful puny."

Next mornin' she woke him up, said, "Stick out your tongue, old man." He stuck his tongue out, and she looked at it hard, said, "Law me! You better stay in the bed today. You must be real sick, from the look of your tongue."

She went and reached up on the fire board, got down all the bottles of medicine and tonic that was there and dosed the old man out of every bottle. Made him stay in the bed several days, and she kept on talkin' to him about how sick he must be. Dosed him every few minutes and wouldn't feed him nothin' but mush.

Came in one mornin', sat down by the bed, and

looked at him real pitiful. Started in snifflin' and wipin' her eyes on her apron, said, "Well, honey, I'll sure miss ye when you're gone." Sniffed some more, said, "I done had your coffin made."

And in a few days she had 'em bring the coffin right in beside the old man's bed. Talked at the old man till she had him thinkin' he was sure enough dead. And finally they laid him out and got everything fixed for the buryin'.

Well, the day that old woman had started a-talkin' her old man into his coffin, the other'n had gone on to her house, and about the time her old man come in from work, she had got out her spinnin' wheel and went to whirlin' it. There wasn't a scrap of wool on the spindle, and the old man finally looked over and took notice of her, said, "What in the world are ye doin', old woman?"

"Spinnin'," she told him, and 'fore he could say anything, she said, "Yes, the finest thread I ever spun. Hit's wool from virgin sheep, and they tell me anybody that's been tellin' his wife any lies can't see the thread."

So the old man come on over there and looked at the spindle, said, "Yes indeed, hit surely is mighty fine thread."

Well, the old woman'd be there at her wheel every time her old man come in from the field—spin and wind, spin and wind, and every now and then take the shuck off the spindle like it was full of thread and lay it in a box. Then one day the old man come in, and she was foolin' with her loom, said, "Got it all warped off today. Just got done threadin' it on the loom." And directly she sat down and started in weavin'—steppin' on the treadles and throwin' the shuttle, and hit empty. The old man'd come and look and tell her what fine cloth it was, and the old woman'd weave right on. Made him think she was workin' day and night. Then one evenin' she took hold on the beam and made the old man help her unwind the cloth.

"Lay it on the table, old man. Look out! You're a-lettin' it drag the floor."

Then she took her scissors and went to cuttin'.

"What you makin', old woman?"

"Makin' you the finest suit of clothes you ever had."

Got out a needle directly and sat down like she was sewin'. And there she was, every time the old man got back to the house, workin' that needle back and forth. So he come in one evenin', and she said to him, "Try on the britches, old man. Here." The old man shucked off his overalls and made like he was puttin' on the new britches.

"Here's your new shirt," she told him, and he pulled off his old one and did his arms this-a-way and that-a-way, gettin' into his fine new shirt. "Button it up, old man." And he put his fingers up to his throat and fiddled 'em right on down.

"Now," she said, "let's see does the coat fit ye." And she come at him with hands up like she was holdin' out his coat for him, so he backed up to her and stuck his arms in his fine new coat.

"Stand off there, now, and let me see is it all right. Yes, it's just fine. You sure do look good."

The old man stood there with nothin' on but his shoes and his hat and his long underwear.

Well, about that time the other old man's funeral was appointed, and everybody in the settlement started for the buryin' ground. The grave was all dug, and the preacher was there, and here come the coffin in a wagon, and finally the crowd started gatherin'. Pretty soon that old man with the fine new suit of clothes come in sight. Well, everybody's eyes popped open, and they didn't know whether they ought to laugh or not, but the kids went to gigglin', and about the time that old man got fairly close, one feller laughed right out, and then they all throwed their heads back and laughed good. The old man tried to tell the folks about his fine new suit of clothes, and then the preacher busted out laughin' and slappin' his knee—and everybody got to laughin' and hollerin' so hard that the dead man sat up to see what was goin' on. Some of 'em broke and ran when the corpse rose up like that, but they saw him start in laughin'—laughed so hard he nearly fell out the coffin—so they all came back to find out what'n-all was goin' on.

The two old women had started in quarrelin' about which one had won the bet, and the man in the coffin heard 'em, and when he could stop laughin' long enough, he told 'em, said, "Don't lay it on me, ladies! He's got me beat a mile!"

Collected by Richard Chase from Kentuckians Maxine Caudell, Bonnie Creech, and Thelma Campbell and published in Chase's *Grandfather Tales* (Boston: Houghton Mifflin, 1948 and 1976).

Br'er Rabbit Chooses His Own Death

An African-American tale about a crafty but lovable trickster

ONE TIME BR'ER FOX PLANTED A GARDENFUL OF HIS favorite food: cabbages. But when Br'er Rabbit came along and saw all those delectable cabbages, he started coming around to eat them every night. That made Br'er Fox mad, so he built a high brush fence all around the garden. Br'er Rabbit paid no attention to it. He clambered over the brush and ate those cabbages same as ever.

Br'er Fox was beginning to mind the loss of those cabbages, so he set a snare for Br'er Rabbit. But that wily ol' rabbit was too smart to get caught, and he just kept on eating.

Br'er Rabbit kept on eating and eating, but good luck makes a body careless. Sure enough, Br'er Rabbit hippity-hopped into the garden one night and—*wham*—got caught in Br'er Fox's snare. There he was when Br'er Fox came down the next morning.

Br'er Fox felt real good, seeing that rabbit hanging there. "He-he, I've got you this time, Br'er Rabbit. Yessir, I've got you this time." Br'er Fox did a little dance around Br'er Rabbit. "This time there's no doubt about it. I'm gonna end your cabbage-thieving days for good. Now, let's see . . . How am I gonna kill you?"

Br'er Rabbit was sure it wasn't his time to die, and he commenced to doing some powerful begging: "Oh, please, good Br'er Fox, I won't take your cabbages anymore."

"Don't I know it," said Br'er Fox. "You aren't gonna take my cabbages anymore because I'm going to kill you."

"Oh, please, Br'er Fox, good Br'er Fox, let me go this time. Cross my heart, I won't steal another one of your cabbages. I swear it."

"Br'er Rabbit, there's no use in your talking. My mind's made up."

"Oh, please . . . " Br'er Rabbit looked real pitiful and sad.

Br'er Fox seemed to be thinking real hard and said at last, "Br'er Rabbit, there's just one thing I'm going to allow you, and that is, I won't kill you the way that is the hardest for you to die. Just tell me what that is, and I'll take some other way."

"Br'er Fox, dying's hard no matter which way you go. But I say the hardest way would be if you took me home and fed me till I was so fat I could hardly move and then turned me out in the deep, deep snow on the first really cold morning."

Br'er Fox allowed that that was a mighty hard way to die, and with a gleam in his eye, he said, "He-he! That's just what I'm going to do to you."

"You said you wouldn't kill me that way," moaned Br'er Rabbit.

"I was just leading you on the whole time, Br'er Rabbit. And now that I know which way is the worst, I'm gonna give it to you."

Br'er Rabbit begged harder and harder, but Br'er Fox paid him no mind. He took Br'er Rabbit home and shut him up in a pen and fed him all he could eat. Well, Br'er Rabbit got so fat that his eyes bulged.

Pretty soon the cold weather started, and every morning Br'er Fox would say, "Is this cold enough, Br'er Rabbit?"

"Naw," Br'er Rabbit would say, "this isn't *half* cold enough. It's got to be really cold."

So it went, morning after morning, but Br'er Rabbit never felt it was cold enough to be put out to die. Br'er Fox started to get uneasy because Br'er Rabbit was eating a whole lot of food. Then one really cold morning came, and Br'er Fox said, "Is this cold enough?"

"Br'er Fox, I don't think it's cold enough . . . er, um, that is, I . . . oh, please, Br'er Fox, don't put me out to die in the snow." Br'er Fox just hummed a happy tune as he pulled Br'er Rabbit out of the pen and dragged him out into the snow. Then he went back and sat on the doorstep to watch him die.

But Br'er Rabbit had no notion that he was going to die just then. He kicked up his feet and hollered out, "You big fool, this weather is just what I've been used to all my life." And off he went into the bushes, *hippity-hop*.

Br'er Fox felt real bad, but what could he do? The snow was so deep that he couldn't run, and Br'er Rabbit got off free as you please.

Adapted by storyteller Sheila Dailey of Mount Pleasant, Michigan, from "How Brer Rabbit Was Allowed to Choose His Death," collected by Gerard Fowks and published in *The Journal of American Folklore,* vol. 1, no. 2 (July–September 1888).

Jack's Good Luck

An Appalachian tale about an adventuresome free spirit

ONCE UPON A TIME, WHEN JACK WAS ABOUT TWELVE OR thirteen years old, he got to thinking about leaving home and getting out on his own like his brothers Tom and Will. But his mama knew he wasn't old enough. "Why do you want to do that?" she'd ask.

"I want to seek my fortune," Jack would answer.

Jack didn't know what a fortune was. He had never seen one or known anybody to find one, and whether it was something that you happened upon or something that happened to you, Jack didn't know. But his curiosity was so powerful that he thought he just had to leave home to seek his fortune.

So his mama said, "Well, Jack, if you've got to go, go on. I'll be here if you need to come back home after a while." Then she packed his clothes and what food she had that would keep, and off went Jack, not knowing what in the world he was looking for.

Jack wandered for about three days, and he soon began to run out of food. So he started looking for a job so he might earn enough to eat while he kept seeking his fortune. But nobody would hire Jack because he didn't have any experience at doing much of anything useful.

Then he met an old farmer whose children were all

grown up and gone. This old man needed help so badly that he was willing to take on anybody—even Jack.

"How much pay do you want?" the farmer asked.

"Oh, I don't exactly know," answered Jack.

When the farmer heard this, he knew he could pull about anything on Jack.

So he said, "I'll tell you, Jack. Since all our children are gone, why don't you come home with me and eat with me and my wife? You can sleep there too. Then whenever you've worked there as long as you want to, I'll pay you whatever wages you've accumulated."

That sounded all right to Jack. More than anything else, he wanted something to eat. So he moved in with the farmer and began to work from daylight to dark six or seven days a week for nothing but his room and board.

Jack worked for a week, then for a month, and before he knew it, a year had passed. Jack worked for two years, then three, and finally he had worked there for seven years without getting paid one cent in real money.

"I believe I've had enough of this," Jack said to himself one day. "I'm not free to seek my fortune as long as I have to work every day. This working is holding me up. I think I'll move on."

That night he told the old farmer that he was leaving and asked him for the wages that he'd been accumulating. The old farmer said, "I'll have them ready for you in the morning."

When Jack sat down to breakfast the next morning, the farmer gave him his seven years of wages. It was a bushel basket just full of money. It was almost all in pennies and nickels and dimes—with just one or two quarters. That basketful must have weighed more than three hundred pounds.

After breakfast Jack said, "I'll be on my way to seek my fortune now," and then he grabbed for that basket. It wouldn't budge. The old farmer and his wife helped

Jack push and pull the basket until he had it out of the house and into the road. Then Jack had it on his own. He worked all day trying to drag the basket of money.

By late in the afternoon he had moved it only a hundred yards toward town. "I'll never be able to find my fortune like this. This money's holding me up." About that time along came a man with a horse and buggy. The buggy was old and so was the horse, but they looked real good to Jack. The man stopped. "What are you doing?" he asked.

"Trying to seek my fortune. But I can't because this money's slowing me down so much."

"What you need is a horse. What would you give me for this fine horse and buggy?"

"I'll give you every bit of this old heavy money," Jack said.

"It's a deal," said the horseman. He could see that there was enough money in the basket to buy at least two pretty good horses. So they made the exchange, and Jack got in the buggy and rode off.

But by the end of the day Jack realized that he was really in trouble. He discovered that he not only had to find a place for himself to sleep and something to eat, but he also had to feed and stable that horse somewhere. That was ten times as hard as taking care of himself, since the horse had to be unhitched and brushed and watered and fed every single day.

Jack thought, "I'm surely going to have to get rid of this horse. It's holding me back from seeking my fortune."

The next morning Jack hitched up his horse, shined up his buggy, and started down the road, anxious to trade. After a while he met a woman who was leading an old cow to market.

"Now that's what I need," thought Jack. "I could have milk to drink whenever I need it. That cow wouldn't have to be curried, and she could sleep anywhere."

So he said to the woman, "I'll trade you a fine horse for that old cow."

"If you throw in the buggy, I'll trade," she said.

Jack was delighted. He handed over the horse and buggy and went on down the road with his cow.

The first time he got thirsty, he found out that the old cow was plumb dry—not a drop of milk for Jack to drink or sell. But that wasn't all. That cow was awful particular about what she ate. Instead of just picking grass along the roadside, she would smell out grain and sweet hay in barns they passed, and it was all Jack could do to keep her from breaking down fences to get to what she smelled.

After about three days Jack had had all he could take. "I'm never going to find my fortune while I'm held up by this old cow," he said. "I'm about ready to trade her for something better."

Just as Jack was thinking this, he saw a man coming down the road with a big fat hen under his arm.

"Now that's what I need," thought Jack. "I'll have an egg to eat every day, and that hen could eat bugs and worms while she followed me along the road."

"Would you trade that old chicken for this fine cow?" asked Jack.

The man was about to wring the hen's neck. But when he saw Jack's cow, he realized that there was a lot more meat on a cow than on a hen.

"I'll swap her for that cow," said the man.

"Done," said Jack, and he started off with his hen.

Well, the hen did lay one egg about two days later, but that was all. And besides, she didn't follow him along the road. Jack had to spend the whole day chasing her over the countryside.

"I can't take this," said Jack. "I'll never be able to seek my fortune with this hen. She's holding me back."

Jack kept on going down the road until he came to a little town, and he stopped at the village blacksmith's shop. He put his hen under his arm and walked right in.

The blacksmith was making nails that day, and Jack was amazed as he watched. Clip, wham, wham, and a nail was made. One after another those nails flew right into a pile on the floor.

"Maybe I need a trade," thought Jack. "That way I could find work from place to place as I go along seeking my fortune." So Jack said to the blacksmith, "I'll give you this fine hen if you'll teach me to make nails."

That blacksmith was awful smart. "I'd like to help you out," he said, "but there's just too many people around here in the nail-making business. What you need is to get into a trade that's not got many people in it. And I've got just the thing you need. You wait right here."

While Jack waited, the blacksmith went out to his garden, which had just been plowed. And in the fresh dirt he soon found what he was looking for: a big yellow flint rock. It weighed about six or seven pounds and was flat on one side. The blacksmith washed it off, oiled the flat side, and took it to Jack. "Here you are, Jack," he said. "This is just what you need, and I'll trade it to you for that old hen."

"What is it?" asked Jack.

"Why, it's a nail-straightening rock. You just hold a crooked nail against it, bent side up, and tap it with a hammer till it's straight. I've had this nail-straightening rock for years and years. It's one of the best. You can make all the money you need with it. Just go up to people's houses and tell them what you're about, and they'll pay all kinds of money to get their nails straightened."

So Jack gave the blacksmith his hen, and he took off with his new nail-straightening rock. On his way down the road to the first house, Jack noticed a well by the roadside. He was thirsty, so he went over to the well, laid his nail-straightening rock down beside him, and dropped the bucket in.

Jack had started pulling up a bucketful of water when

his elbow accidentally hit the nail-straightening rock and knocked it clear into the well. It went down into the darkness, out of sight. His nail-straightening rock was gone.

Jacked reared back and threw out his chest. "I reckon I must be the luckiest man in the world," he said to himself. "I've been held up by a seven-year job, a basketful of money, a horse and buggy, an old cow, a wild hen, and a nail-straightening rock. But now there's not one thing in the world to hold me back. At last I'm really free to seek my fortune."

And off went Jack, unburdened, on his way.

Told from his family tradition by storyteller Donald Davis of Ocracoke Island, North Carolina, and appears in Davis's *Jack Always Seeks His Fortune* (Little Rock, Ark.: August House, 1992).

Epaminondas and His Auntie

An African-American folk tale about the difficulty of following instructions

EPAMINONDAS USED TO GO TO SEE HIS AUNTIE MOST EVERY day, and she nearly always gave him something to take home to his mammy. One day she gave him a big piece of cake—nice yellow rich-gold cake.

Epaminondas took it in his fist and held it all scrunched up tight and came along home. By the time he got home, there wasn't anything left but a fistful of crumbs.

His mammy said, "What you got there, Epaminondas?"

"Cake, Mammy," said Epaminondas.

"Cake!" said his mammy. "Epaminondas, you ain't got the sense you was born with! That's no way to carry cake. The way to carry cake is to wrap it all up nice in some leaves and put it in your hat and put your hat on your head and come along home. You hear me, Epaminondas?"

"Yes, Mammy," said Epaminondas.

The next day Epaminondas went to see his auntie, and she gave him a pound of butter for his mammy—fine fresh sweet butter.

Epaminondas wrapped it up in leaves and put it in his hat and put his hat on his head and came along home.

It was a very hot day. Pretty soon the butter began to melt. It melted and melted, and as it melted, it ran down Epaminondas's forehead; then it ran over his face and in his ears and down his neck. When he got home, all the butter Epaminondas had was *on him.*

His mammy looked at him, and then she said, "Law's sake! Epaminondas, what you got in your hat?"

"Butter, Mammy," said Epaminondas. "Auntie gave it to me."

"Butter!" said his mammy. "Epaminondas, you ain't got the sense you was born with! Don't you know that's no way to carry butter? The way to carry butter is to wrap it up in some leaves and take it down to the brook and cool it in the water and cool it in the water and cool it in the water and then take it in your hands, careful, and bring it along home."

"Yes, Mammy," said Epaminondas.

By and by, on another day, Epaminondas went to see his auntie again, and this time she gave him a little new puppy dog to take home.

Epaminondas put it in some leaves and took it down to the brook, and there he cooled it in the water and cooled it in the water and cooled it in the water; then he took it in his hands and came along home. When he got home, the puppy dog was cold and shivering.

His mammy looked at it, and she said, "Law's sake! Epaminondas, what you got there?"

"A puppy dog, Mammy," said Epaminondas.

"A *puppy dog*!" said his mammy. "My gracious sakes alive, Epaminondas, you ain't got the sense you was born with! That ain't the way to carry a puppy dog! The way to carry a puppy dog is to take a long piece of string and tie one end of it around the puppy dog's neck and put the puppy dog on the ground and take hold of the other end of the string and come along home."

"All right, Mammy," said Epaminondas.

The next day Epaminondas went to see his auntie

again, and she gave him a loaf of bread to carry to his mammy—a fresh brown crusty loaf.

So Epaminondas tied a string around the end of the loaf and took hold of the end of the string and came along home. When he got home his mammy looked at the thing on the end of the string, and she said, "My laws a-mercy! Epaminondas, what you got on the end of that string?"

"Bread, Mammy," said Epaminondas. "Auntie gave it to me."

"Bread!" said his mammy. "Oh, Epaminondas, Epaminondas, you ain't got the sense you was born with; you never did have the sense you was born with; you never will have the sense you was born with! Now I ain't gonna tell you any more ways to bring truck home. And don't you go see your auntie, neither. I'll go see her my own self.

"I'll just tell you one thing, Epaminondas! You see these six mince pies I done made? You see how I done set 'em on the doorstep to cool? Well, now, you hear me, Epaminondas: *you be careful how you step on those pies!*"

"Yes, Mammy," said Epaminondas.

Then Epaminondas's mammy put on her bonnet and her shawl and took a basket in her hand and went away to see auntie. The six mince pies sat cooling in a row on the doorstep.

And then—and then—Epaminondas *was* careful how he stepped on those pies! He stepped—right—in—the—middle—of—every—one.

Collected and adapted from the African-American tradition by Sara Cone Bryant and published in Bryant's *Epaminondas and His Auntie* (Boston: Houghton Mifflin, 1907, 1935, and 1938).

Jack Goes to Seek His Fortune

An Appalachian tale about an enterprising young man and his animal helpers

ONE TIME THERE WAS A LITTLE BOY NAMED JACK. HIS mother was dead, and his father had married again, but his stepmother didn't like Jack and was mean to him.

So one day Jack decided he would leave home and go out in the world to seek his fortune. So he started out. He hadn't gone but a little piece when he met a horse.

"Good morning, Jack," said the horse, "where are you going?"

"Going to seek my fortune," said Jack.

"May I go with you?" said the horse.

"Yes," said Jack, "the more the merrier." So Jack and the horse went on. Hadn't gone but a little piece when they met a cow.

"Good morning, Jack," said the cow, "where are you going?"

"Going to seek my fortune," said Jack.

"May I go with you?" said the cow.

"Yes," said Jack, "the more the merrier." So Jack and the horse and the cow went on. Hadn't gone but a little piece when they met a dog.

"Good morning, Jack," said the dog, "where are you going?"

"Going to seek my fortune," said Jack.

"May I go with you?" said the dog.

"Yes," said Jack, "the more the merrier." So Jack and the horse and the cow and the dog went on. Hadn't gone but a little piece when they met a ram.

"Good morning, Jack," said the ram, "where are you going?"

"Going to seek my fortune," said Jack.

"May I go with you?" said the ram.

"Yes," said Jack, "the more the merrier." So Jack and the horse and the cow and the dog and the ram went on. Hadn't gone but a little piece when they met a rooster.

"Good morning, Jack," said the rooster, "where are you going?"

"Going to seek my fortune," said Jack.

"May I go with you?" said the rooster.

"Yes," said Jack, "the more the merrier." So Jack and the horse and the cow and the dog and the ram and the rooster went on. Hadn't gone but a little piece when they met a cat.

"Good morning, Jack," said the cat, "where are you going?"

"Going to seek my fortune," said Jack.

"May I go with you?" said the cat.

"Yes," said Jack, "the more the merrier." So Jack and the horse and the cow and the dog and the ram and the rooster and the cat went on. Hadn't gone but a little piece when they met a goose.

"Good morning, Jack," said the goose, "where are you going?"

"Going to seek my fortune," said Jack.

"May I go with you?" said the goose.

"Yes," said Jack, "the more the merrier." So Jack and the horse and the cow and the dog and the ram and the rooster and the cat and the goose went on.

They went on and on, traveled all day. Long about sundown they began to look for a place to stay all night.

They was in an awful wild and thinly settled country and hadn't seen nobody for a long time. At last they come to a big house sittin' way up on the side of a hill with a big high fence around it. They went up to the house and found that nobody lived there and decided to put up in it for the night.

So Jack put the horse just inside the gate, the cow just outside, and he told them not to let anyone come in. Then he put the ram on the porch and the goose just inside the door and the cat on the hearth and the dog under the bed and the rooster up on top of the house. Then he pulled off his things and went to bed.

It was a robbers' meeting place, but Jack didn't know it. The robbers had stored a lot of money there that they had robbed people of in the countryside and the towns around there.

So way long in the night the robbers come. They thought somebody might be around, so two of them waited down the road a little piece and sent the other one to investigate. He slipped up to the gate, and just as he got there, the cow picked him up on her horns and tossed him over the gate. The horse kicked him onto the porch. The ram butted him through the door. The goose flapped him with her wings and bit him. He ran to the fireplace to make a light, and the cat scratched him. He ran under the bed, and the dog bit him. And as he jumped through the window and started running, the rooster began crowing for day.

When the feller got back to his buddies, he was nearly dead. They wanted to know what was the matter. He told them he slipped up to the gate and that a farmer there pitched him over the gate with a pitchfork, and a blacksmith there struck him with a sledgehammer and knocked him onto the porch. A rail-maker there struck him with his maul and knocked him through the door. There also stood a thrasherman, and he like to flailed him to death with his flail. He run over to the fireplace to start a light, and there was an old woman sitting on the hearth, a-sewing, and she stuck her needle in him. He went to hide under the bed, but there was a shoemaker under there, and he stuck his awl in him. He made it to the window and jumped out, and as he ran away, he heard the leader of them all up on the top of the house, hollering, "When you get through with him, send him to me."

So the robbers was afraid to go back to the house, and next morning Jack looked over the place and found their gold. He took it and bought hay for the horse and cow, bones for the dog, milk for the cat, and corn for the ram and the goose and the rooster. Then Jack married him a wife, and they all lived happy.

Collected by James Taylor Adams from Lenore Corene Kilgore in 1940 through the Virginia Writers' Project and published in Charles L. Perdue Jr.'s *Outwitting the Devil* (Santa Fe, N.M.: Ancient City Press, 1987).

Big Man Jack Killed Seven at a Whack

An Appalachian story of a crafty but reluctant hero

WELL, JACK AND HIS MOTHER WAS SEEING IT HARD, SO he got out a-hunting for a job. He was a-walking along, and he come to three forks of a road. So he said, "I'm a-gonna throw my hat up, and whichever way the air takes it, that's the road I'm a-going." It went in the right-hand road, so he took it.

He hadn't gone too far till he'd picked up a piece of wood and was a-whittling on it. And the first thing he knowed, he had a paddle made. He come to a mudhole in the road, and butterflies had lit all over it, a-sucking it. He whacked down with that paddle he'd hewed out and killed seven.

He went on his way, and he met a man who said the king had put out word that there was a wild boar out a-doing lots of damage—killing people and cattle. A unicorn was out doing lots of damage too. This got on Jack's mind, and he went on to a blacksmith man and had a big leather belt made and put reading on it: BIG MAN JACK KILLED SEVEN AT A WHACK! Didn't say what—it was just seven butterflies—just said BIG MAN JACK KILLED SEVEN AT A WHACK!

So he went on and started inquiring and found the king of that country and hollered him out. Jack said, "I've heard you've got out word that there's a wild boar a-doing lots of damage and that a lot of people had got hurt trying to kill it and some got killed." The king said, "Yeah, but," he said, "the way you look . . . it'll live on and do more damage." Jack said, "Well, bedad, if that's the way you feel about it," and he turned around to walk off.

When he turned around, the king caught the reading on his belt. The king said, "Wait a minute here!" Said, "What's that on your belt?" The king looked at it. He said, "Big Man Jack Killed Seven at a Whack! Oh," he said, "wait! You're the man I'm a-needing!" Said, "Great goodness!" Said, "Are you up to what's on your belt?" Jack said, "Yeah, I'm up to it." So the king said, "Well," said, "come on in, and we'll eat supper, and tomorrow morning we'll try you out."

Well, next morning come, and they eat breakfast, and he took Jack on a horse where they last said the boar was seen. He let Jack off, and it was a sight to see that king whip his horse, a-feared that it would get onto him before he got out of there. Jack said, "Well, bedad," he said. "Now my life is in danger!" Said, "If hit's that dangerous, the way he whipped that horse, I might better slip out of here and go back on what I've got on my belt."

Well, he started trying to slip out, but that old wild boar smelled him, and it come a-knocking, its tushes a-cutting big trenches outen the trees, and got after him. Directly it got so close on him that the only way Jack saw to save his life was to head for a little old log house he saw way down in a holler, with the roof rottened off of it. So he took out, and by the time he got to it and started to climb the logs over in it, the wild boar was so close till it bit off a corner of his coat-tail. Then the wild boar run in at the doorway to try to reach up to get him, and Jack jumped back outside and propped the door good, where the wild boar couldn't get out. He checked it good and took off for the king's house.

King come out and said, "Did you do any good?" Jack

said, "I don't know whether I done any good or not." He said, "I got up there just a few minutes after you left, and something like a little old shoat come out, with things out of its mouth about six inches long." Said, "Me and hit got to playing, and hit got a little mad, directly, and bit the corner of my coat-tail off. I just flew a little mad too, so I picked it up by the tail and ears and shoved it in a little old log building up there." Said, "You can go see if that's what it is."

So the king ordered up his men and rifles. But when they went, the king's men saw it and wouldn't get close enough to shoot it. Jack grabbed a rifle and sighted, and when he shot, it was so big that it just tore down that whole little old building. When they cleaned it out, it cleaned up to eight wagon-loads of meat, and the king give Jack $500 as a reward for killing it.

The king said, "Well, now," said, "being you've done so good, hit's a unicorn a-doing lots of damage too." Jack was a-dreading it. But the king took him the next morning and left him where they said they'd last seen it. Jack said, "Bedad, I've got $500 in my little old ragged pocket. I could spend that and get the good out of it. But," he said, "I'm going to mess around here yet and get killed and lose it all. I believe I'll see if I can slip out of here." So he got to trying to slip out of there, but the unicorn smelled him.

And that horn on the end of its forehead, it begin to size at him, and Jack got to dodging this way and that way behind the trees. Finally the unicorn got worried so that it made a dive and just centered a big tree and stuck that horn plumb through it and wedged it. Jack took a switch and whipped it to see if it could get loose. It was so big till it was nearly a-grubbing that big tree. He decided he better not switch it much but just ought to hurry on to the king.

So he went on to the king. The king said, "Did you see anything?" Jack said, "Gosh," he said, "I got up there just a little while after you let me off, and something come at me. It looked kindly like a horse, but it had a little old horn of a spike on its forehead." Said, "Me and hit got to playing a little bit, and it got to sizing at me, like it was wanting to hurt me." Said, "I just grabbed it up by its head and tail and stove that horn through a tree and wedged it to hold it there. You can take your men and see if that's what it is."

So the king went, and the men too, and they wouldn't get near hit to shoot it. Jack took a sight on it, and when he shot it, it was so big that it grubbed that tree when it fell. They skinned hit out and got its hide and saved it and went back. The king paid Jack another $500, and Jack started home—and was glad of it. Had a thousand dollars, and he was out of it.

He hadn't got around the road but a little ways till the men of the community had sent in word that they was a lion had got out. The king said to 'em, "Huh," said, "great goodness! Why couldn't you have come a little earlier?" Said, "My man that killed the unicorn and the hog has done gone. I've paid him off. But," said, "it could be that I could overtake him."

So the king overtook Jack, and Jack saw he could make a raise on it. The king said, "There's a lion out, and you're the man for it!" Jack said, "Well," said, "I don't know that I'll go back for what I done the others for." The king said, "I'll give you a thousand." Said, "I'll boost it five." So Jack took him up on it, and the king took him where they told him they'd seen it. The king rode away.

Jack said, "Now, me with a thousand in my little ragged pocket . . . " Said, "That's awful, to tackle a wild lion. I better see if I can slip out of here!" So Jack got to trying to slip out, but the lion smelled him. It roared so big, it started rock a-rolling off the mountain. It come on and got so close, Jack had to climb a great big old poplar tree. So the lion began to gnaw, trying to gnaw it down. That tree was so big till the lion give out in its jaws and lay down and went to sleep. And didn't lack but about a third of having the tree down where it would fall.

Jack's heart was a-beating in his neck. He decided he'd better see if he could slip down and get out over that lion while it was asleep. So he started slipping down the tree but got his foot on a brickle limb and started sliding and hit right on the lion's back. That woke the lion up and excited it, and it just started out running with Jack on its back. It run and got in the courthouse, where they was a-having court. Well, they got out word to the king's men that Jack was in there on the lion and couldn't get off and was a-running around there, had them all scared to death.

The king's men got there before the king got there. And they kept on trying to get a shot and get the lion but couldn't to keep from hitting Jack. Finally they got a aim and shot the lion. And it was running so fast till when they shot it, it stoved Jack's head and shoulders in the ground. And by that time the king had got there.

Jack rose up off the ground, a-brushing the mud off. He said, "King," said, "now look what your men has done!" The king said, "What do you mean?" Jack said, "I had that lion trained for a ridey-horse." Said, "They've had to up and shoot it! You'd a-looked big, a-riding around over the country, a-riding a lion in place of a horse!" Said, "And these men has shot it."

The king flew mad off of it, and he said, "All right, now, men," he said, "I would a-looked big. It's just like Jack said. I'd a-liked to have rid that." And said, "You men has got to boost Jack $500 for shooting that lion." So they boosted it $500, and that made him two thousand and five hundred dollars. And him and his mother lived pretty good for a while off of that.

Collected from Ray Hicks of Banner Elk, North Carolina, and recorded on the album *Ray Hicks* (Sharon, Conn.: Folk-Legacy Records, 1963).

The Three Piggies

A Kentucky version of a favorite children's story

ONE TIME THERE WAS AN OLD SOW WHO HAD THREE PIGS: Tom, Will, and Jack. They got up great big, and the old sow turned them out to live for themselves.

Tom said, "Mommy, I'm goin' to build me a house."

She said, "I'm afeard you're goin' to get caught."

"No, I won't. I'll build it out of stick and straw."

He was buildin' on his house one day when he saw a fox a-comin'.

"What're you doin', little pig?"

"Buildin' me a house."

"I'll come to see ye when ye get it built."

"All right."

Tom got his house built, and he looked out and saw the fox a-comin'. He jumped in the house and shut the door. The fox came and said, "Let me in, little pig."

"In my nose, in my tail, I shan't do it."

"If you don't let me in, I'll get on top of your house, and I'll shickel and shackel and tear it down." The fox got on top of Tom's house, and he shickeled and shackeled and tore it down, and he caught the pig and ate him.

Well, Will said, "Mommy, I'm goin' to build me a house."

She said, "No, you'll get catched like your brother."

"No, I won't. I'll build it out of wood."

He went out, and he was buildin' on his house when he saw the fox a-comin'. The fox said, "What are you doin', little pig?"

"Buildin' me a house."

"I'll come to see ye when ye get it built."

"All right."

Will got his house built, and he saw the fox a-comin'.

"Let me in, little pig."

"In my nose, in my tail, I shan't do it."

"If you don't let me in, I'll get on top of your house and shickel and shackel and tear it down." The fox got up on top of Will's house, and he shickeled and shackeled, and he tore it down and caught the pig and ate him.

Jack said, "Mother, I'm goin' to build me a house."

She said, "No, you must not. You'll get catched like your two brothers."

"No, I won't. I'll build it out of brick."

Jack was buildin' on his house when he saw the fox a-comin'.

"What're you doin', little pig?"

"Buildin' me a house."

"I'll come to see ye when ye get it built."

"All right."

Jack got his house built and looked out and saw the fox a-comin'.

"Let me in, little pig."

"In my nose, in my tail, I shan't do it."

"If you don't let me in, I'll get on top of your house, and I'll shickel and shackel and tear it down."

The fox got on top of Jack's house, and he shickeled and shackeled, but he couldn't tear it down. He got back down and came to the door and said, "Let my nose in, little pig, I'm a-freezin'."

Jack let the fox's nose in.

"Let my head in, little pig, I'm a-freezin'."

Jack let his head in.

"Let my forelegs in, little pig, I'm a-freezin'."

Jack let his forelegs in.

"Let my body in, little pig, I'm a-freezin'."

Jack let his body in.

"Let my hind legs in, little pig, I'm a-freezin'."

Jack let his hind legs in.

"Let my tail in, little pig, I'm a-freezin'."

Jack let his tail in.

The old fox jumped up and down and shouted, "Piggie and peas for my supper! Ha-ha!"

Then the little pig said to him, "Law me, Mr. Fox, I see a man and a gun, and he's got a great gang of greyhounds a-comin'."

"Where will I go, where will I go?"

"Jump right here in my chest, and I'll lock you up."

So the fox jumped in the chest, and Jack locked him up. Then Jack put on a kettle of water. The fox said, "What are you heatin' that water for, little pig?"

"Gonna make you some tea."

"That's right, little piggie, that's right."

Then Jack went to borin' a hole right down through the top of the chest.

"What're you borin' that hole for, little pig?"

"To give you some air."

"That's right, little piggie, that's right."

Then Jack went to pourin' that boilin' water on him through the hole. The fox yelled, "Ouch, Jack, I'm gettin' hot! I'm gettin' hot!"

And that was the last of the fox. Jack burnt him up.

Collected by Leonard Roberts and published in Roberts's *Sang Branch Settlers: Folksongs and Tales of a Kentucky Mountain Family* (Austin, Texas: University of Texas Press in conjunction with the American Folklore Society, 1974).

Br'er Tiger and the Big Wind

An African-American tale about cleverly righting a wrong

IN OLDEN DAYS THE CREATURES USED TO PLOW IN THE fields and plant their crops the same as menfolks. When the rains came, the crops were good. But one year no rain came, and there was a famine in the land. The sun boiled down like a red ball of fire. All the creeks and ditches and springs dried up. All the fruit on the trees shriveled, and there was no food or drinking water for the creatures. It was a terrible time.

But there was one place where there was plenty of food and a spring that never ran dry. It was called the Clayton field. In the field stood a big pear tree, just a-hanging down with juicy pears, enough for everybody.

So the poor hungry creatures went over to the field to get something to eat and something to drink. But a great big Bengal tiger lived under the pear tree, and when the creatures came nigh, he rose up and said, "Wumpf! Wumpf! I'll eat you up. I'll eat you up if you come here!" All the creatures backed off and crawled to the edge of the woods and sat there with misery in their eyes, looking at the field. They were so starved and so parched that their ribs showed through their hides, and their tongues hung out of their mouths.

Now, just about that time, along came Br'er Rabbit, just a-hopping and a-skipping as if he'd never been hungry or thirsty in his life.

"Say, what's the matter with you creatures?" asked Br'er Rabbit.

"We're hungry and thirsty and can't find any food or water—that's what's the matter with us," answered the creatures. "And we can't get into Clayton field because Br'er Tiger said he'd eat us up if we came over there."

"That's not right," said Br'er Rabbit. "It's not right for one animal to have it all and the rest to have nothing. Come here. Come close. I'm going to tell you something." And Br'er Rabbit jumped up on a stump so that all could see him as they crowded around. When Br'er Rabbit had finished whispering his plan, he said, "Now, you all be at your posts in the morning; everyone be there before sunup."

The first animal to get to his post was Br'er Bear. Before daybreak he came, toting a big club on his shoulder, and took his place alongside an old hollow log. The next creature to arrive was Br'er Alligator Cooter, a snapping turtle, who crawled in the hollow log. Then Br'er Turkey Buzzard, Br'er Eagle, Br'er Chicken Hawk, and all the other big fowls of the air came a-sailing in and roosted in the tops of the tall trees. Next to arrive were the tree-climbing animals, like Br'er Raccoon and his family and Sis Possum and all her little ones. They climbed into the low trees. Then followed the littler creatures, like Br'er Squirrel, Br'er Muskrat, Br'er Otter, and all kinds of birds. They all took their posts and waited for Br'er Rabbit.

Pretty soon, when the sun was about a half-hour high, along came Br'er Rabbit down the big road, with a long grass rope wrapped around his shoulder. He was just a-singing: "Oh, Lord, oh, Lord, there's a great big wind that's a-coming through the woods, and it's going to blow all the people off the earth!" And while he was singing his song, a powerful noise broke out in the woods.

There was Br'er Bear a-beating on the hollow log with

all his might: *bic-a-bam, bic-a-bam, bic-a-bam, bam, bam!* Inside the log Br'er Alligator Cooter was a-jumping: *bic-a-boom, bic-a-boom, bic-a-boom, boom, boom!* Br'er Turkey Buzzard, Br'er Eagle, and Br'er Chicken Hawk were a-flapping their wings and a-shaking the big trees, and the trees were a-bending, and the leaves were a-flying. Br'er Raccoon and Sis Possum were stirring up a fuss in the low trees, while the littler creatures were a-shaking all the bushes. On the ground and amongst the leaves the teeny-weeny creatures were a-scrambling around. All in all, it sounded like a cyclone was a-coming through the woods!

All this racket so early in the morning woke Br'er Tiger out of a deep sleep, and he rushed to the big road to see what was going on. "What's going on out there, huh?" he growled. "What's going on out there?"

All the creatures were too scared to say anything to Br'er Tiger. They just looked at him and hollered for Br'er Rabbit to "Tie me! Please, sir, tie me!"

Now, all this time Br'er Rabbit just kept a-hollering: "There's a great big cyclone a-coming through the woods that's going to blow all the people off the earth!" And the animals just kept a-making their noise and a-hollering, "Tie me, Br'er Rabbit. Tie me."

When Br'er Rabbit came around by Br'er Tiger, Br'er Tiger roared out, "Br'er Rabbit, I want you to tie me. I don't want the big wind to blow me off the earth!"

"I don't have time to tie you, Br'er Tiger. I've got to go down the road to tie those other folks to keep the wind from blowing them off the earth. It sure looks to me like a great big hurricane is a-coming through these woods."

Br'er Tiger looked toward the woods, where Br'er Bear was a-beating, and Br'er Cooter was a-jumping, and the birds were a-flapping, and the trees were a-bending, and the leaves were a-flying, and the bushes were a-shaking, and the wind was a-blowing—and it seemed to him as if Judgment Day had come.

Old Br'er Tiger was so scared he couldn't move. He said to Br'er Rabbit, "Look here! I've got my head up against this pine tree. It won't take but a minute to tie me to it. Please tie me, Br'er Rabbit. Tie me, because I don't want the wind to blow me off the face of the earth."

Br'er Rabbit shook his head. "Br'er Tiger, I don't have time to bother with you. I told you, I have to go tie those other folks."

"I don't care about those other folks," said Br'er Tiger. "I want you to tie me so the wind won't blow me off the earth. Look, Br'er Rabbit, I've got my head here against this tree. Please, sir, tie me."

"All right, Br'er Tiger. Just hold still a minute, and I'll take time to save your striped hide," said Br'er Rabbit.

Now, while all this talking was going on, the noise kept getting louder and louder. Somewhere back yonder it sounded like thunder was a-rolling! Br'er Bear was still a-beating on a log: *bic-a-bam, bic-a-bam, bic-a-bam bam, bam!* Br'er Cooter was still a-jumping on the log: *bic-a-boom, bic-a-boom, bic-a-boom, boom, boom!* And the birds were a-flapping, and the trees were a-bending, and the leaves were a-flying, and the bushes were a-shaking, and the creatures were a-crying—and Br'er Rabbit was a-tying!

He wrapped the rope around Br'er Tiger's neck, and he pulled it tight; he wrapped it around Br'er Tiger's feet, and he pulled it tight. Then Br'er Tiger tried to pitch and rear, and he asked Br'er Rabbit to tie him a little tighter, "because I don't want the big wind to blow me off the earth." So Br'er Rabbit wrapped him around and around so tight that even the biggest cyclone in the world couldn't blow him away. And then Br'er Rabbit backed off and looked at Br'er Tiger.

When he saw that Br'er Tiger couldn't move, Br'er Rabbit called out, "Hush your fuss, children! Stop all of your crying! Come down here—I want to show you something. Look. There's our great Br'er Tiger. He had all the pears and all the drinking water and all of everything, enough for everybody, but he wouldn't give a bite of food or a drop of water to anybody, no matter how much they needed it. So now, Br'er Tiger, you just stay there until those ropes drop off you. And you, children, gather up your croker sacks and water buckets. Get all the pears and drinking water you want, because the Good Lord doesn't love a stingy man. He put the food and water here for all his creatures to enjoy."

After the animals had filled their sacks and buckets, they all joined in a song of thanks for their leader, Br'er Rabbit, who had shown them how to work together to defeat their enemy, Br'er Tiger.

Collected by William J. Faulkner from former slave Simon Brown of the Gullah tradition of South Carolina and published in Faulkner's *The Days When the Animals Talked* (Chicago: Follet, 1977).

Jack the Woodchopper

A Virginia tale about a kindhearted boy who reaps great rewards

ONE TIME THERE WAS AN OLD WOMAN, AND SHE HAD three sons. The youngest son was named Jack, and Jack was a good boy, but his brothers were mean and didn't like to mind their mother. Now, this old woman was a widow and awful poor.

They kept getting poorer and poorer all the time. So the old woman told the oldest boy he'd have to go into the forest and cut wood and sell it to get something for them to live on. He didn't want to go, but he finally went off muttering, carrying a piece of cake and a bottle of wine, nearly the last the old woman had.

So he went on till he came to an old man sittin' on a log. He was very old and looked awful hungry. He said, "My boy, won't you divide your food with me?"

"No, sir," said the oldest boy, "I've only got a piece of cake and a bottle of wine, and come to think of it, I'm hungry." So he eat his cake and drank his wine with the old man sittin' there watching him and never offered him a bite. He went on and started chopping wood, and the first tree fell on him and broke his legs, and they had to come and carry him home, a cripple for life.

So the old woman sent her second son. He went off muttering to himself and carrying the last piece of cake and last bottle of sweet wine. He went on till he come to where the old man was sittin' on a log. The old man hailed him and said, "My boy, won't you give me a little of your cake and wine? I'm awful hungry."

"I have nothing to spare beggars," the boy said, and he eat his cake and drank his wine and started chopping wood. Hadn't chopped but a few licks when he cut his foot and had to be carried home, a cripple for life.

So the old woman said to her youngest boy, "Jack, you'll have to go and chop wood so we may have something to live on." So Jack started out, but all he had to take with him was a crust of bread and a few sups of sour wine in a bottle. So he went on and found the old man sittin' on the log. "Give me something to eat, my boy, I'm starving," the old man said to Jack.

Jack was tenderhearted, so he give the old man half of his crust and half of his wine, and as soon as he took it, his part and Jack's turned into a fine cake and a full bottle of sweet wine, and they had a good meal. Then the old man pointed to a tree and told Jack if he would chop away the roots, he would find something that would bring him good luck all his days. So Jack chopped away the roots of the tree and found a golden goose.

So Jack took the golden goose and started home. Hadn't gone far when he met up with three girls. One of them ran up and started to stroke the goose, but she stuck to it and couldn't get loose. Another one of the girls tried to pull her loose, but she stuck to her. Then the third one tried to pull her loose, but she stuck to her. So they started out, Jack carrying his goose, and the girls following behind him.

So they went, and they met up with three preachers. One of them began shaming the girls for following a poor woodchopper and told them to leave him and come with them to church. They kept right on after Jack, and the old preacher walked up and laid his hand on the last girl's shoulder, and his hand stuck to her, so he started on after them. The other two preachers began calling for him to come on with them, and one ran up and grabbed him by the shoulder, and his hand stuck to him. Then the third preacher grabbed him, and he stuck to him, so they all went on, following Jack and his golden goose.

So they all went on and had to pass the king's house. Now, the king had a daughter who had never smiled and he had offered to let her marry any man who would make her smile. This girl was standing at her window, looking out, and saw Jack pass by, leading all those people behind his golden goose, and it looked so funny that she smiled.

The old king thought Jack had done that to make her smile, so he sent for Jack to come in. And when Jack went in, the king told him he'd made his daughter smile, but before he'd let Jack marry her, there was one more thing he had to do. He would have to find somebody who could eat a thousand loaves of bread at one time.

Jack thought that would be impossible, and he left and went out in the woods. There he found a man sittin' on a log with all kinds of bread scraps lyin' around him. He was just tightening up his belt. He told Jack he'd eaten all the bread he could find and was still hungry. So Jack told him to come and go with him, and he took him to the king's house, and there all stacked up was a thousand loaves. The man started in on 'em and eat 'em all up right now.

So the old king called Jack in and told him that there was one more thing Jack would have to do before he'd let him marry his daughter. He'd have to find somebody who could drink a thousand bottles of wine at one time.

Jack thought it would be impossible to find such a man, and he went off in the woods. There he found a man with parched lips sittin' by the path and all sorts of wine bottles lying empty around him. He told Jack he'd drunk all the wine he could find, but he could not quench his thirst. So Jack told him to follow him, and he took him to the old king's house. There was a thousand bottles of wine, and this fellow drank them right down.

Then the old king told Jack there was one more thing he'd have to do before he'd let Jack marry his daughter. He'd have to find a ship that would sail on both land and water.

Well, Jack thought that was impossible. So he left and went out in the woods. There he met up with the old man who had give him the golden goose. He said, "What troubles you, Jack?" And Jack told him that he had to find a ship that would sail on land as well as on water before the old king would give him his daughter for a wife.

Well, the old man took out his knife and started whittling. In no time he had whittled out a ship. The ship started growing, and right away it was a big ship. Jack got in it, and it sailed away over the road and across the river and come to the king's house.

When the old king saw Jack and his ship, he give him his daughter, and they were married and sailed away across the ocean. They were gone several years, and when they went back, the old king was dead, and Jack become king and his wife was the queen, and they lived happy.

Collected by James Taylor Adams from Spencer Adams in 1941 through the Virginia Writers' Project and published in Charles L. Perdue Jr.'s *Outwitting the Devil* (Santa Fe, N.M.: Ancient City Press, 1987).

Nippy and the Yankee Doodle

An Appalachian relative of "Jack and the Beanstalk"

ONCE THERE WAS AN OLD WOMAN WHO HAD THREE SONS named Jim, John, and Nippy. One weekend Jim and John told their mother to bake them a cake because they was going to see their girls. Nippy, the youngest and the one they thought foolish, spoke up and said, "Let me go with you."

And they said, "No, you're a foolish boy, and you had better stay at home with your mama." When they started out, Nippy went to his mother and said, "Mommy, bake me a cake. I want to go and foller my brothers."

And she said, "All right, Nippy, if you'll take the riddle [sieve] and go down to the spring and get me a riddleful of water, I'll bake you a cake." She thought this would be a way to keep him at home.

He went down to the spring with the riddle, dipped it up full of water, and started back. The water all poured out, of course, right on through it. He'd dip it up again, and it'd pour out. He tried it several times and never got started with any water. Then he heard a little bird up on a tree, said:

Daub it with moss, and slick it with clay,
And you can carry your water away.

He looked up and said, "What did you say, little bird?" The bird said:

Daub it with moss, and slick it with clay,
And you can carry your water away.

So he daubed the riddle with moss and then slicked it over good with clay, filled it up with water, and went to the house. His mother thought he had done a smart trick, so she baked him a big cake and put it in a poke and let him set out, follering his brothers. Caught up with 'em that evening, and that night they went to see an old man's three daughters who lived by the river.

The next morning the oldest boy, Jim, wanted to marry the man's oldest daughter, and the old man said, "I'll tell ye what I'll do." Said, "You go over to that old man's house across the river and get his three gold lockets and his gold staff, and I'll let you marry my oldest daughter."

So all three of them went across the river where the old man lived and asked to stay all night. He let 'em come in and stay. He had three daughters, and they all slept on pallets on the floor—the girls on one side and the boys on the other. Nippy was kindly scared and stayed awake till way along in the night.

Sometime before the fire went out, the old man come in. He brought three gold lockets and put 'em around his three girls' necks and then eased out of the room. Nippy saw what he was doing and was afraid the man would come back in and kill the ones who didn't have gold lockets on. So when everything got quiet again, he eased over and took the gold lockets off the girls' necks and put 'em on his and his brothers' necks.

Later in the night the old man come in and cut his three daughters' throats. The next morning, right at the edge of daylight, why, Nippy got his brothers up, and they took the three lockets and the old man's gold staff and headed back across the river. About the time they got across the river, the old man come to the edge of the river and called, "Hey, Nippy, when are you comin' back?" Said, "You've caused me to kill my three girls, and you've stole my three gold lockets and my gold staff. When are you coming back to see me?"

Nippy said, "I'll be back sometime, Grandpa."

They went on into the house, and Jim married the man's oldest daughter. Sometime the next day John wanted to marry the next oldest daughter, so the man said, "I'll tell you what I'll do." Said, "If you'll go over the river to the old man's and get his half-moon, I'll give you two yoke of oxen, a half a bushel of gold, and my daughter."

The next day the older boys talked around about how foolhardy Nippy was and got him to go over by himself. He went over there to get the half-moon. The old man wasn't at home, but his old woman was there, making hominy. He had to wait around awhile to get that half-moon. When the old woman went out of the room, Nippy eased up on the roof and started pouring salt down the fire. The fire started crackling and burning blue blazes. The old man come in about that time, smelled around, and said, "Old woman, you're burnin' your hominy up." She grabbed the half-moon and run to look at her hominy, and Nippy pushed her in the fire, grabbed the half-moon, and headed back across the river with it.

Time he got across the river, the old man run to the edge and hollered at him, said, "Hey, Nippy, when are you comin' back to see me?" Said, "You caused me to kill my three girls, you stole my three lockets and my gold staff, and now you've pushed my old woman in the fire and gone with my half-moon." Said, "When are you comin' back?"

He said, "I'll be back to see you again, Grandpa."

He took the half-moon in and give it to the old man. His brother John got the two yoke of oxen, the half bushel of gold, and the next oldest daughter.

After the celebration Nippy decided he wanted to marry the youngest daughter, so he asked the old man for her. The old man said, "Tell ye what I'll do." Said, "I'll give you two yoke of oxen, a half bushel of gold, and my youngest daughter if you'll go back over to that old man's house and get his Yankee Doodle [a musical instrument]."

So Nippy went over after the Yankee Doodle that evening. The old man and the old woman were gone to church, and about the time Nippy got it and started back, he saw them coming. So he hid under the bed with the Yankee Doodle. Along after dark, when the old man and the old woman went to bed, he started playing on the Yankee Doodle under there. The old woman said, "Old man, you're getting awful good all at once." Said, "You just get back from church and start playing the Yankee Doodle."

He said, "Why, old woman, I've not thought of that Yankee Doodle in forty years."

She said, "Well, Nippy must be around again."

So the old man reached under the bed and pulled Nippy out, said, "I've got you this time, Nippy."

Nippy said, "What are you goin' to do with me, Grandpa?"

He said, "I'm goin' to kill ye!"

Nippy said, "I wouldn't do that if I was you, Grandpa." Said, "If I had you, I'd put ye up in the loft and feed ye on eggs and butter till you got right fat and then kill ye and invite all the neighbors in for a feast."

The old man said, "Well, that's just what I'll do with you, Nippy."

So he put him up in the loft and fed him on eggs and butter for about two weeks and decided he was fat enough to kill. Then he went up and said, "Well, you're fat enough to kill now, Nippy. I'm goin' to lay you on the coolin' board."

Nippy said, "You don't have to take time to kill me, Grandpa." Said, "I'm easy killed, and Grandma can do that while you go and invite all the neighbors in."

The old man said, "All right, that's what I'll do, Nippy." Said, "I'll go and invite all the neighbors and tell her to pop you in the oven for a feast."

So Grandma put on the clay oven to get it right real hot. She kept going to look at the oven to see if it was hot enough. Nippy waited till it got real hot, and when she went the next time, he slipped up behind her and pushed her in the oven and popped the lid on her. Then he grabbed the Yankee Doodle and took back out across the river.

The old man come along about that time with some hungry neighbors, saw what Nippy had done. Said, "Hey, Nippy, when are you comin' back to see me?" Said, "You caused me to kill my three daughters, you stole my three gold lockets and my gold staff, you pushed my old woman in the fire and stole my half-moon, and now you've killed my old woman and stole my Yankee Doodle." Said, "When are you comin' back to see me?"

Nippy said, "I don't guess I'll ever be back to see ye, Grandpa." He took the Yankee Doodle back to the old man and got his two yoke of oxen, the half bushel of gold, and the youngest daughter to marry.

Nippy played the Yankee Doodle while they all danced and celebrated their weddings. Then he and his brothers took their oxen and their gold and their wives home, built houses, settled down, and lived happy ever after.

Collected by Leonard Roberts from Lige Gay of Dry Hill, Kentucky, and published in Roberts's *Nippy and the Yankee Doodle and Other Authentic Folk Tales From the Southern Mountains* (Berea, Ky.: Council of the Southern Mountains, 1958).

How the Terrapin Beat the Rabbit

A Native American version of "The Tortoise and the Hare"

THE RABBIT WAS A GREAT RUNNER, AND EVERYBODY KNEW it. No one thought the terrapin anything but a slow traveler, but he was a great warrior and very boastful, and the two were always disputing about their speed. At last they agreed to decide the matter by a race. They fixed the day and the starting place and arranged to run across four mountain ridges, and the one who came in first at the end was to be the winner.

The rabbit felt so sure of himself that he said to the terrapin, "You know you can't run. You can never win the race, so I'll give you the first ridge, and then you'll have only three to cross while I go over four."

The terrapin said that would be all right, but that night when he went home to his family, he sent for his terrapin friends and told them he wanted their help. He said he knew he could not outrun the rabbit, but he wanted to stop the rabbit's boasting. He explained his plan to his friends, and they agreed to help him.

When the day came, all the animals were there to see the race. The rabbit was with them, but the terrapin had gone ahead toward the first ridge as they had arranged, and they could hardly see him on account of the long grass. The word was given, and the rabbit started off with long jumps up the mountain, expecting to win the race before the terrapin could get down the other side. But before he got up the mountain, he saw the terrapin go over the ridge ahead of him.

He ran on, and when he reached the top, he looked all around but could not see the terrapin on account of the long grass. He kept on down the mountain and began to climb the second ridge, but when he looked up again, there was the terrapin just going over the top.

Now he was surprised, and he made his longest jumps in order to catch up. But when he got to the top, there was the terrapin away in front, going over the third ridge. The rabbit was getting tired now and was nearly out of breath, but he kept on down the mountain and up the other ridge until he got to the top—just in time to see the terrapin cross the fourth ridge and thus win the race.

The rabbit could not make another jump, and he fell to the ground, crying "Mi, mi, mi, mi," as the rabbit has done ever since when he is too tired to run anymore. The race was given to the terrapin, and all the other animals wondered how he'd won against the rabbit, but he kept still and never told anyone.

It was easy enough, however, because all the terrapin's friends looked just alike, and he had simply posted one of his friends near the top of each ridge to wait until the rabbit came in sight and then to climb over and hide in the long grass. When the rabbit came on, he could not find the terrapin and so thought that the terrapin was ahead. Even if he had met one of the other terrapins, he would have thought it the same as the first one because they looked so much alike. The real terrapin had posted himself on the fourth ridge so as to come in at the end of the race and be ready to answer questions if the animals suspected anything.

Because the rabbit had to lie down and lose the race, the conjurer nowadays, when preparing his young men for ball play, boils a lot of rabbit hamstrings into a soup and sends someone at night to pour it across the path along which the other players will come in the morning, so that they may become tired in the same way the rabbit did and lose the game. It is not always easy to do this because the other party is expecting it and has watchers sent ahead to prevent it.

Collected by James Mooney and published in the *Nineteenth Annual Report of the Bureau of American Ethnology to the Secretary of the Smithsonian Institution 1897–98*, part 1, by J.W. Powell (Washington, D.C.: Government Printing Office, 1900; republished, St. Clair Shores, Mich.: Scholarly Press, 1970).

Old Drye Frye

A lighthearted Appalachian tale with a simple refrain: everybody knows Old Drye Frye

ONCE THERE WAS A PREACHER NAMED OLD DRYE FRYE. HE wasn't famous or nothing, and all he'd ever get paid was what came out of the collection plate and a chicken dinner after the service.

Once he was over at a house, eating his chicken dinner, when he got a chicken bone stuck in his throat, and be-darned if he didn't choke to death right at the table. "Oh, Lord," said the man, "Old Drye Frye's dead, and if he gets found here, they'll hang me for murder for sure."

So he picked Old Drye Frye up and carried him over to the neighbor's and propped him up against the front door. Directly someone came and opened the door, and Old Drye Frye fell in. "It's Old Drye Frye" (everybody knows Old Dry Frye), the man of the house said. "And he's dead as a door nail. If he's found here, they'll hang me for murder for sure."

So he picked up Old Drye Frye and carried him down the road a piece and set him up against the side of the road. A bunch of men came along and saw him and thought he was a robber. So they started throwing rocks at him until one of 'em said, "I do believe it's Old Drye Frye" (everybody knows Old Drye Frye). "If he's found dead here, everybody'll blame us, on account of they know we've been walking this stretch of road."

So they picked Old Drye Frye up and carried him over and set him up against a neighboring farmer's corncrib. Well, when the farmer woke up in the morning, he saw a man by his corncrib. He was mad because people had been stealing his corn. So the farmer shouted, "Get away from that corncrib, or I'll shoot you." Old Drye Frye didn't move a muscle, so the farmer filled him full of birdshot.

"Oh, Lord," he said, "I do believe I shot Old Drye Frye" (everybody knows Old Drye Frye). "Now I done killed him, and they'll get me for murder for sure."

He carried Old Drye Frye into his corncrib and left him sitting there till that night. When the moon went down, he carried him over to the river, where they did the baptizing, and he figured people would find him the next day. He sat Old Drye Frye on a rock, with his elbows sitting on his knees and his head a-laying in his hands. He looked just as natural as you please sitting there.

Early the next day a boy came down to the river and saw Old Drye Frye sitting there. "Mornin', Mr. Frye," said the boy (everybody knows Old Drye Frye). "How you doing?" Old Drye Frye didn't say nothing. Well, that boy was full of the devil and just as feisty as you please, so he said, "I said, 'Howdy, Old Drye Frye.' Ain't you going to say hello?" You see, that boy didn't care how he talked to anybody. Old Drye Frye just sat there and didn't say nothing.

"Looky here, Drye Frye, if you don't say howdy, I'm gonna knock you a good one." Drye Frye just sat there and didn't answer. So the boy hit him a good lick, and Old Drye Frye tumbled right into a deep pool in the river.

He thought they'd get him for murder, so when everybody started coming down for the big baptizing, he just sat in the back of the meeting and didn't say nothing.

The people arrived, and nobody could figure out where Old Drye Frye was. Someone allowed as how he'd been over to their place for dinner just a couple of nights ago. Somebody else told how they'd seen him resting along the road. When he didn't show up, they sang a couple of hymns and took up a collection, and then everybody went home, and that mischievous boy went home too.

Late that night he hooked Drye Frye out of the river pool and stuffed him in a sack and carried him down the road. He was going to hide him somewhere out in the woods. The boy was toting the sack down the road when he came upon a couple of men who'd been out stealing hogs. They were carrying their sacks and lit out for the woods. The boy found the sacks that the robbers had dropped. So he left Old Drye Frye lying there and took a sack of hogs and went home.

Later the robbers came back and picked up their sacks and went on home. They hung the sacks in the smokehouse and went to bed.

The next morning the lady of the house went out to the smokehouse to cut some meat. She cut open one of the sacks and out fell . . . old Drye Frye. Well, her hollering woke up half the county, and she knocked the smokehouse door off its hinges getting out of there.

The robbers went in to see what was the matter. One of them said, "I swear, it's Old Drye Frye" (everybody knows Old Drye Frye). "How'd he get here? We got to get shot of him, or they'll get us for murder."

There were some wild horses on their land, so they rounded one of 'em up. That night they put a no-account bridle and saddle on it, tied Old Drye Frye to the saddle, tied his hands to the saddle horn, and stuck an old hat on his head. Then they opened all the gates and let the horse go. That horse shot out of there and danced down the road with that preacher bouncing along on top of him.

Then the rogues ran out of the barn, yelling, "Stop, thief! He's done stole our horse. Stop him! Horse thief!"

All the neighbors came out of their houses, hollering and shouting, but none of 'em could stop that horse and his rider. He jumped a fence and headed up the mountain, running toward Kentucky. And as far as I know, Old Drye Frye and that horse are running still.

Told by Giles Asbury and published in John Harrell's *A Storyteller's Treasury* (Berkeley, Calif.: York House, 1977).

Wicked John and the Devil

An Appalachian tale about a man mean enough to beat the devil at his own game

MANY YEARS AGO THERE WAS A MAN NAMED JOHN WHO lived in the mountains of North Carolina. Ever'body called him Wicked John 'cause that's just what he was—one of the wickedest men you'll ever lay eyes on. Old John was mean and stingy and just downright hateful. He was so mean, even his wife was scared of him. Wicked John was a blacksmith by trade, and folks did say that he was a mighty, mighty fine blacksmith.

Ever' mornin' Wicked John would get up and yell down to his wife, "Woman, is my breakfast ready?"

And his wife would say, "Yes, Wicked John," and then she'd run off into the closet and lock herself in.

Old Wicked John would stomp down the stairs and over to the table and eat just as quickly as he could. When he finished, he would get up and walk down the road to his blacksmith shop. As he stood in front of the locked door, he would pull a set of keys from his pocket, open the door, prop it open, go into the shop, and prepare his work for the day.

One day as Wicked John unlocked the door and propped it open, he all of a sudden saw a bright and shining glow in the back of the shop. That made Wicked John a little angry, so he yelled, "Who's that back there in my shop?"

All of a sudden the light cleared, and standing there was an angel, and the angel said, "Good mornin', Wicked John."

Wicked John said, "Who are you?"

The angel said, "Wicked John, I have come to give you three wishes."

"Wishes?" said Wicked John. "Wishes? I don't want your wishes. Get out of my shop."

"Well," said the angel, "we've been watchin' you, and we know that you're an awfully unkind man, and if you don't take these wishes, you won't go to heaven when you die."

"Listen here," said Wicked John, "if you don't get out right now . . . just look at you, droppin' them feathers all over my shop. Get on out of here."

But the angel said, "I can't leave until you take the wishes."

"Wishes?" said Wicked John. "All right. I'll take the wishes. Now let me see. Wishes . . . wishes . . . I know exactly what I want to wish for. Do you see that hammer over there? Well, that hammer is what I work with every day, and every time I start to work in my blacksmith shop, men come up from town and get to messin' and feelin' and touchin' my work, especially my hammer. Well, I want to put on that hammer a wish that if anybody touches it, that hammer sticks to 'em, and they won't be able to turn it loose until I say so."

The angel said, "What an awful wish."

Wicked John said, "But that's my wish. Do I get it or don't I?"

"So be it," the angel said. "You have your first wish. But be very careful. For you see, you have only two more."

"Well," said Wicked John, "I've got me another wish. Every time I finish work here in my blacksmith shop, I go home in the afternoon to get a chance to sit on my porch a spell before suppertime. Well, somebody's always a-sittin' in my favorite chair. I wish that anybody I catch sittin' in my chair won't be able to get outa it till I say so."

The angel said, "Good heavens. That's an awful wish."

"It's my wish. Do I get it or don't I?"

"Oh yes," said the angel. "So be it. You have one more wish."

"Huh . . . huh . . . huh . . . Well, I'll tell ya," said Wicked John. "I make plenty of money here in this blacksmith shop, and I put it all right here in my pocketbook, and then I put my pocketbook in my pocket. When I go home, I put my pocketbook on the dresser. My wife drags my money out of my pocketbook and says she's got to buy this and she's got to buy that. I never can keep my money. I want to wish that any money I put in my pocketbook won't be able to come out 'less I say so or until I'm dead."

"Oh," the angel said. "What an awful wish."

"It's mine. Now, do I get it or don't I?"

The angel said, "So be it."

And the angel disappeared.

Wicked John lived on, and he got meaner and meaner and meaner. One day he walked down to the blacksmith shop, unlocked the door, and propped it open, and sure enough, he saw a bright and shining glow. Wicked John said, "Who's that back there in my shop?"

The light cleared away, and there standing before Wicked John was the devil himself. Wicked John said, "How do you do? What do you want?"

And the devil cackled and said, "I want *you*."

"Please," Wicked John said. "Can't I finish my work?"

The devil said, "No, you can't. I'm ready to take you now."

"But I've got to work," said Wicked John. "You see,

I'm a man that's known for gittin' all of his work done, and I've got to keep on workin'."

The devil said, "You oughta thought about that a hundred years ago when you was bein' mean. I'm goin' to take you away from here. You's makin' my name somethin' awful here on earth."

Wicked John said, "All right. I know I've got to go with you, so if you'll just let me finish my work, I'll go easily."

The devil laughed and said, "Hurry up."

Well, Wicked John went to work, but he worked slower and slower and slower, and soon the devil got madder and madder and madder, and after a while the devil said, "Listen here. I'm ready to go."

Wicked John said, "Well, if you want me to go, maybe you can help me work."

"All right," the devil said. "What do you want me to do?"

Wicked John said, "You can help me do some hammerin'."

The devil said, "Where's the hammer?"

Wicked John said, "Right over there on the table."

The devil walked over and took a look at the hammer. Well, the hammer was big, and it looked heavy, so the devil thought he oughta pick it up with both hands, and he did. He tried to hand it to Wicked John, but the hammer didn't move. It just stuck to the ol' devil.

"Turn me loose," said the devil. "Turn me loose."

Wicked John asked, "Havin' a little problem there?"

The devil said, "You know I am. You know I am. You get me offa this hammer."

Wicked John said, "I'll be glad to, but you've got to make a little bargain with me."

The devil said, "Bargain? Bargain? I don't bargain with the likes of you."

Wicked John said, "Well, you can stay on that hammer then."

"All right," said the devil. "What kind of bargain do you want me to make with you?"

Wicked John said, "I want you to go away, and don't come back botherin' me no more."

The devil said, "I can't do that. I done promised myself that I's goin' to take you offa this earth, and your soul's goin' to be mine. I'm stuck to ya. But I'll tell you what. I'll go away for twenty years, and at the end of twenty years, I'm comin' back to get you, and I ain't pickin' up no hammers neither."

Wicked John said, "Is that the best you can do?"

The devil said, "You can take it or leave it."

"Well," said Wicked John. "All right. Drop the hammer."

The devil dropped the hammer from his hands, lifted himself up into the air, turned around fifteen times, and took off.

Wicked John lived on, and he got meaner and meaner and meaner. He got so mean that his wife hardly ever came out of the closet. Twenty years went by, and Wicked John retired from the blacksmith shop. He went home, and every day he'd sit in his rockin' chair on his front porch and rock. Wicked John was an old man, and he couldn't see too good. He was too stubborn to buy 'im a set of glasses, so he just sat there and rocked.

One mornin' he was lookin' down the road, and he couldn't see who was comin'. All he saw was a shadow. But he could hear the ol' devil's cackle, and Wicked John knew right then and there who it was. Well, that shadow came to the house, put his foot up on the porch, and said, "Howdy, Johnny."

And Wicked John said, "Devil, it must be you."

The devil said, "Yeah, it's me. Now come on. Let's go. Twenty years is up."

"Oh," Wicked John said, "I know twenty years is up, and I might as well go with ya. But I'm an old man, and it's gon' take me a while to pack my clothes."

The devil said, "Pack your clothes? You don't need no clothes. Just get you some short-sleeve shirts, and let's go."

"All right," Wicked John said. "But it's gon' take me a little while to find them short-sleeve shirts. I don't see so good. While I'm gone, why don't you rest here in my rockin' chair, and I'll come back when I get my shirts all packed."

The devil said, "Hurry up."

Wicked John went in and stayed and stayed and stayed. After a while the devil got tired of waitin', so he got up and walked over to the door. But when he got up, the chair got up with 'im. The devil was stuck to the chair, and he screamed, "Git me outa here." He lifted 'imself offa the ground and ripped the front porch and roof right offa the house. Old Wicked John stuck his head out the front door and said, "Havin' a little problem there?"

The devil said, "You know I am. You get me outa here."

"All right," said Wicked John. "I'll get you outa there, but you've got to make a little bargain with me."

The devil said, "There you go again. Bargains, bargains. I done told ya. I don't bargain with the likes of you."

"Well," said Wicked John, "you can just take me on then, but that chair will go with you."

"All right," said the devil. "I know what you want. You want me to go away again, but you see, you ain't got twenty years left. I'll go away this time for five years, but at the end of them five years, I'm comin' back, and I ain't pickin' up no hammers, and I ain't sittin' in no chairs."

Wicked John said, "Is that the best you can do?"

The devil said, "Take it or leave it."

"All right," said Wicked John. "Drop the chair."

And the devil dropped the chair, lifted into the air,

turned around twenty times, and took off.

Wicked John lived on, and he got meaner and meaner and meaner. One day five years later Wicked John was takin' his mornin' walk. The old man's eyesight had completely gone. He was so blind he had to walk with two canes. He was goin' down the road, walkin' along, when somebody stopped right beside 'im. He couldn't see who it was, but he could hear 'im cackle, and he could smell brimstone, so right away he knew.

Wicked John said, "Mornin', Devil. I know that's you."

The devil laughed. "You're goin' in the right direction, Johnny. Keep a-movin'."

"I know I can't fight you no longer," said Wicked John. "I'll just keep a-goin' like I am."

The devil and Wicked John walked down the road, and the devil was so proud and happy that he finally had Wicked John's soul that he commenced to kickin' dust into Wicked John's face, and Wicked John began coughin'.

The devil said, "What's wrong with you?"

Wicked John said, "Look at ya. You're kickin' that dust and dirt into my face, and it's gittin' my throat all dry. I need to get the dust outa my throat so I can go on."

The devil said, "Well, get it out."

But Wicked John said, "I need me a cold drink."

The devil said, "Where do you expect to get it?"

"I ain't sure where we are," said Wicked John. "You know, I don't see so good, but is that a store across the road?"

The devil said, "Yeah, it is."

"I'll tell you what," Wicked John said. "I'll go over there and get me a cold drink, and when I get the dust and dirt outa my throat, I'll be able to go right on home with ya."

The devil said, "Well, hurry up."

So Wicked John started across the road. But all at once he stopped right in his tracks, turned around, and faced the devil. "Listen here," he said. "I was comin' outa my house so fast this mornin' that I forgot to pick up my money and put it in my pocketbook. I ain't got no money. Would you loan me a quarter?"

The devil just cackled and said, "I ain't got no quarter."

"Oh," said Wicked John, "what am I gonna do?" Then he thought for a minute. "I'll tell you what," said Wicked John. "They tell me that you can turn yourself into any shape or form that you want."

The devil laughed and said, "That's right."

Wicked John said, "Well, why don't you turn yourself into a quarter and jump up here in my hand? I'll put you in my pocketbook, go into the store, and get myself a cold drink. Then you can turn yourself into a gnat and fly on back out here, and we can just go on home."

The devil said, "That's a good idea. I should've thought of that one myself."

With that, he leaped up into the air, turned around twenty-five times, and fell back into Wicked John's hand as a quarter. Wicked John opened his pocketbook, dropped in the quarter, closed the pocketbook, laughed to himself, and went on back home.

Everything would have been fine, but Wicked John was an old man and didn't live long. Within six months he died in his sleep one night. All the neighbors came to see 'im, and somebody spied Wicked John's pocketbook there on the dresser and wanted to know how much money the old man had saved up. One of the neighbors opened John's pocketbook, and out flew the devil. They tell me he's been flyin' round ever since.

Told from her family tradition by storyteller Jackie Torrence of Salisbury, North Carolina—one of many variants that exist.